Blue Laws, Brahmins, – & – Breakdown Lanes

An Alphabetic Guide
To Boston and Bostonians

by
Karen Cord Taylor

illustrations by Gil Fahey

D0044043

The Globe Pequot Press □ Chester, Connecticut

Copyright © 1989 by Karen Cord Taylor

Library of Congress Cataloging-in-Publication Data
Taylor, Karen Cord
    Blue laws, brahmins, and breakdown lanes : an alphabetic guide to Boston and Bostonians / by Karen Cord Taylor. — 1st ed.
      p   cm.
  ISBN 0–87106–648–3
    1. Boston (Mass.)—Civilization.   I. Title.
F73.52.T38   1989   89–11822
974.4'61—dc20   CIP

Manufactured in the United States of America
First Edition/First Printing

TO DAN, LESLIE, AND SUSANNAH

About the Author

Karen Cord Taylor grew up near Champaign, Illinois and has lived in Berkeley, California; Cambridge, Massachusetts; and Washington, D.C. Since she moved to Boston twenty years ago, she has caught a burglar with her bare hands and spent 1,170 hours looking for parking places. She has replaced three trees in front of her house and painted seventy-three rooms. She has observed a gunfight and suffered a stolen car and four break-ins. She has won a home-remodeling contest sponsored by a local bank and a citation for the flowers she tends in a narrow alley at the side of her house.

Ms. Taylor has written more than fifty articles for magazines and newspapers. She is also co-author, with Doris Cole, A.I.A., of *Howe, Manning & Almy—Stylish Creators of America's Past* (Midmarch Arts Press). The book tells of three architects, women, who practiced in their own firm in Boston for forty years in the early part of this century.

Ms. Taylor writes speeches and articles for executives, and she produces brochures and newsletters for professional organizations and businesses. She lives in Boston with her husband and two children.

Preface

I wrote this book because I thought you might want to know about Boston. I don't mean the Boston of the Freedom Trail or Old Ironsides, although those sights are interesting enough. The face of this city has been well documented over hundreds of years and I don't plan to repeat those performances. I feel less· strongly about Boston's face than about its heart. What gives this city life? What makes it tick?

The city's heart is its people. How do Bostonians live? Why do they act as they do? What is it about Boston that comforts or annoys them? How do they regard their fellow citizens? How do the city's history, climate, and physical character affect those who live there?

In answering these questions, we come upon several undeniable themes. Parking problems, traffic hassles, disorganization, a frustrating absence of logic, fragmentation, suspicion, street trash, and a touch of arrogance torment a Bostonian's spirit. People everywhere suffer from at least some of these afflictions, but this city seems to struggle with them more often and with greater intensity. Why, then, if life here is so difficult, do people find the city so satisfying?

Part of the answer must lie in Boston's rich resources for art and the mind, its history, its dignity, and its traditionalism, which afford its visitors and its residents substance and a refuge from capricious trends.

But I think the rest of the answer is simpler. People grow to love Boston because, if the heart of a city is its people, then Boston has more of a heart, even if it misses a beat now and then. I don't mean that people here are better or wiser or deeper or kinder. I mean literally that more people are in downtown Boston at all hours of the day and night than is usual in many American cities. Even at the height of suburban popularity Bostonians didn't use the city only as a stage for work and then take off to their real lives twenty miles away. We didn't call our downtown the "inner" city (remember that label?) and abandon it to the poor and powerless. Here we mixed it up among the poor, the middle class, and even the rich, who hung in, living downtown until the place became fashionable once again. Although many businesses sprang up in the suburbs, the financial community and the center of business life stayed. The best shopping, the most interesting restaurants, the most desirable cultural activities, the most beloved sports remained in Boston Proper. The center of this city is a real center. It's where people want to be.

If we live here now, we feel it. The downtown residential neighborhoods are once again the most desirable in the metropolitan area. Downtown is alive. Lights shine through windows. The sidewalks are full of people. Visitors can feel safety in the numbers out with them on the streets. All this company doesn't mean we're free of poverty, crime, police corruption, and some of the same problems other cities have. Concentrating uses in the center does mean that our traffic problems are worse than in cities in which uses are dispersed. But Boston Proper has a vitality and an appeal that continues to make Bostonians believe they live at the center of the world.

I've arranged the book by phrases or words that Bostonians use frequently or will recognize easily. They are in alphabetical order because that is the easiest way. In getting to the city's heart, I've relied on facts, when available, and information gleaned from experts in the field. Boston fascinates the people who know it well. My experts, listed in the Acknowledgments, were enormously helpful and, contradicting the typical Bostonian's reputation, generous with their time and knowledge. I want them to know how much I appreciate their taking time from jobs or leisure to add to the accuracy and the flavor of this book.

Though based on objective information this book, however, is ultimately the product of opinion. The opinion is mine, gleaned from two decades of reading the newspapers, walking around, making friends, looking for a parking place, writing about the city, watching the magnolias bloom, taking the T, sweeping the sidewalk, raising children, voting, following the Celtics, picking up trash, running red lights, chasing burglars, and involving myself in the life of this deeply layered, old, intelligent, often frustrating city.

A **ccent.** *Pahk the cah in Hahvud Yahd.* That
may not be all you need to know about the
way Boston talks, but it's a good start. Bostonians don't take an *r* into account unless it's not there,
as in *What's the big idear?* If they sew, they use a *PAT -
nnn*. They ignore middle consonants. They call contemporary life *mau - nnn*. Broad *a* reigns supreme
here. Bostonians take *bahths* and eat *tomahtoes* and
they're not putting you on. They would never confuse
their mother's sister's title with the name of an insect.
Linguists say that, as you might expect, the Boston
accent has its roots in the British accent back in the
colonial period.

For a while elocution teachers and ministers tried to
spread the Boston upper-class accent through the rest
of the country as the one to emulate in fine speaking.
Even though the effects of this effort lasted through the
1930s, at least in the movies, it didn't take with the
general population.

Boston's strong identification with an accent doesn't
mean that we all talk alike. An old Boston Brahmin
sounds different from an old politician from South Boston. But their children, with accents more like standard
American, sound different from both of them. Besieged
by television and newcomers, the Boston accent's days
may be numbered. It may become as much of an
anachronism as the favorite example for showing it off:
It's been a long time since anyone was able to park a
car in Harvard Yard.

4

Across the River. Students and professors at Boston University use this expression resignedly. Harvard is across the river. Neither Boston University nor any other institution of higher learning in the Boston area will ever match Harvard in influence and prestige. Cantabrigians (people who live in Cambridge) use the phrase to state the emotional difference between the Harvard on the Cambridge side of the river and the Harvard Business School on the Boston side. With its concentration on crass commercialism, should Harvard Business School be considered worthy of the same name as the rest of the university?

Consulting is a big industry *across the river.* And so, for the men and women who work downtown, *across the river* is where the experts hang out—at M.I.T. and Harvard. It doesn't matter to them that the Harvard Business School, which offers some of the most celebrated advice, is technically *not* across the river; business people downtown use *across the river* in bafflement and awe. If the business community is not baffled and awed by the advice they've purchased, they will be once they get the bill.

Adaptive Reuse. Ever since a nineteenth-century developer tore down John Hancock's Beacon Street house to build a couple of brownstones, Bostonians have debated the merits of destroying a building or keeping it. The advantages of tearing down: new buildings, inevitably larger, allow Boston businesses to expand vertically within the cramped downtown. The advantages of keeping a building: the old buildings have scale, design, and color that are distinctive to Boston. Their presence preserves the ancient street patterns and the pedestrian accessibility that have made this city's downtown one in which people actually want to live, as well as work.

A compromise of sorts has been worked out over the past few years, overseen by the Boston Redevelopment Authority. New buildings have been built. The downtown has found ways to expand that don't require demolition—over the Mass. Pike, into the old rail yards across the Fort Point Channel, and to Kendall Square in Cambridge, which is no farther from Boston's Financial District than the Back Bay. A number of old buildings have been saved and turned to new uses, sometimes adding a story or two. Churches, wharf buildings, and a spaghetti factory are now residential condominiums. The old Natural History Museum is the home of a clothing store. Old City Hall is an office building with a restaurant. The former Federal Reserve Bank is a hotel. The old produce and meat center, Quincy Market, became Faneuil Hall Marketplace—Bostonians still call it Quincy Market—predicted to be too cute for the natives, but frequented by the natives anyway.

Everyone, including the much-maligned high-rise developer, loves most of the old buildings in Boston. After a few disasters, the prevailing wisdom is now that if people love a building, it is better to save it. If the whole building can't be saved, then it is better to save at least the façade. If a new building does replace an old one, it must blend in with, not stand out from, the design and dimensions of the older buildings around it. A story has made the rounds and every one believes it. The architect for Rowes Wharf, a 1980s complex thought to be one of the best newer buildings in the city, was told, "That's a wonderful rehab." He knew he had received the highest compliment a Bostonian could bestow.

Alewives. A kind of herring that come to Massachusetts coastal ponds and rivers, including the Charles, to spawn in the spring. You'll find the name on bodies of water, roads, MBTA stops, and even office parks. The alewife, not the cod, was the most readily available source of food for the Pilgrims. Since colonial times these fish also have been used as bait for lobsters and stripers (striped bass). Alewives are oily and don't dry as well as cod, but old-timers bake them fresh or pickle them. Those really in the know strip the tasty roe from the fish and throw the carcass into a hill of corn as fertilizer, a trick the Indians reputedly taught the Pilgrims. Alewives have long been more plentiful in Massachusetts than in more southern states because colonial laws, enforced intermittently to this day, required that fish ladders be built on all rivers and brooks where dams or mills were constructed.

With overfishing, acid rain, polluted waters, and periods of inattention to the fish ladders, it's a wonder any kind of herring survived here. But they did, and the herring run, including that of the alewives, is a big show in May, particularly amid the gentle terrain on the South Shore and the Cape. The tourists who stumble onto the scene can't believe the sight of all those slippery silver bodies fighting their way upstream. They say you can walk across the river on the fishes' backs, but you probably won't see any one try it. Catching any kind of herring is regulated by the towns, and so those who would go fishing must check with town officials before getting out their nets. Some towns establish "catching" days, when town wardens catch the fish and sell them by the bushel.

The catch has been improving in Massachusetts because, like everywhere else, we are cleaning up our rivers. With improving water quality and controls on catch size, other fish like the salmon and shad, the largest herring—called the "poor man's salmon," a name hard to fathom because aficionados are convinced the shad and its roe are far tastier—are returning to Massachusetts rivers.

Ancient and Honorables. In 1638, Governor Winthrop chartered a military organization to defend the Massachusetts Bay Colony in case of attack by Indians or rioting within. The place having turned out to be fairly calm for almost 150 years, the military organization found itself with little to do. It kept up appearances anyway. By 1738, it was known as the Ancient and Honorable Artillery Company of Massachusetts. It did not distinguish itself in the Revolutionary War and, as a body, has served in no war since.

The Ancient and Honorables and their 700 or so members now reside on the top floor of Faneuil Hall, their home since 1746. They call themselves the oldest chartered military organization in the world. Their duties are to dress up in full regalia, display their armory to the public, put on parades, show up for the commission ceremony with the governor on the first Monday in June, and take a fall tour of duty to a foreign land. Recent forays, which must be approved by the State and Defense Departments, have been to Munich, Rome, and Beijing.

Now, by tradition, every important Massachusetts public ceremony includes the Ancient and Honorables. James Michael Curley reportedly proclaimed the Ancient and Honorables, "Invincible in peace. Invisible in war." It's the perfect military organization.

Anglophilia. Afternoon tea, the town house, the venerable London Harness Company, governesses, boarding schools, gentlemen's clubs, the love of the cultured landscape so beautifully exhibited at Mt. Auburn Cemetery, the accent, and toleration of inedible food. Though Bostonians were quick to get rid of the King, we've had a hard time in some quarters throwing off everything else English.

Part of this bias is historic economics. After the Revolution, Boston merchants found they shared manufacturing and shipping interests with some English cities. They established special relationships with London investment bankers that fueled growth in New England. Boston shippers bitterly opposed the War of 1812 and considered seceding from the Union at that time.

Common economic interests fostered a continuing exchange of visitors and culture between Boston and English cities. Early in the nineteenth century it became fashionable among the upper classes to emulate life among the English gentry with elegant country and city houses, a large circle of friends and visitors, and a fleet of carriages and horses as well as sailing boats. Successful Boston merchants formed the Boston Athenaeum, taking as their model the private gentlemen's library in Liverpool, a prosperous English merchant and shipping city, thought to be like Boston. About the only discouraging word about England came from Dr. Oliver Wendell Holmes, who criticized unscientific English medical practices and the food. He preferred France for both. But Holmes was called the "Improper Bostonian" by one biographer and may not have been representative of general feeling.

The presumed threat that accompanied arrival in Boston of Irish immigrants by the thousands probably intensified the earlier arrivals' loyalty to England. Today, the major economic tie that binds Boston to Britain is Masterpiece Theatre, the only television show cultured Bostonians will admit to watching.

Anglophobia. For every Bostonian who exhibits Anglophilia, two will display Anglophobia. The latter have excellent historical company all the way back to Sam Adams and his friends. Boston was an appropriate place for the Irish, for during the Revolution it was the first American city to throw off the English yoke. The Boston Irish have been trying to do for the rest of the world what the patriots did for Boston ever since. Among the more interesting efforts was the Fenian Movement. After the Civil War, Irish soldiers who had seen how effective they could be at freeing the slaves decided they might as well free Canada too. On two occasions several hundred men gathered near the Canadian border to make the attempt. In 1870, about forty Irishmen from Boston took the train to St. Albans, Vermont, where they met with the small liberating force. They crossed into Canada and did battle with the Canadians, who didn't seem to appreciate the help in ridding them of British oppression. These exploits were covered by John Boyle O'Reilly, a reporter for the *Boston Pilot,* a Catholic newspaper that continues to this day. For a few moments after the general leading the Fenians was arrested by United States officials, O'Reilly, later the *Pilot's* editor, was put in charge of the exploit. This event, coupled with his peculiar death at an early age, added to the mythological aura he ultimately attained.

More recently, the Boston Irish have spent more energy fretting about Northern Ireland than about Canada. The message from Boston to England has been the same as in the Revolutionary War: "Get out."

Antiques. Like the nineteenth century Boston lady and her hat ("Where do you buy your hats," asked a New York visitor. "My dear, we don't buy our hats," said the Boston dowager, "We already have them.") the most Boston of Bostonians don't buy antiques. They have them, preferably made in colonial times or brought back from Asia in great-great-great grandfather's ship. Everyone else, whose ancestor had not the foresight to bring back heirlooms during the China Trade, must make do with what's available at the better auction houses, suburban shops, or around Charles or Newbury streets. Only the stuff made before 1850 is prized. English pieces of the same vintage are only second best, but have the advantage of being more plentiful. The English at that time weren't building a country and so had more time and money to spend on furniture than Americans, who were busy buying ploughs and waterworks. Victoriana, so popular in the rest of the country, clearly is third best here.

Asher Benjamin. The work left by architect Asher Benjamin allows Bostonians to tell the American architecture story from the Boston point of view. Benjamin inherited Bulfinch's unofficial position as architect laureate of Boston. He designed the Charles Street Meeting House, Old West Church, and early houses on Beacon Hill. He also published the 1797 *Country Builder's Assistant,* the first pattern book of architecture published in the United States. It and its subsequent editions and variations helped establish Benjamin and his carefully executed Greek Revival details as the predominant influence on American domestic architecture for the first half of the 1800s. Greek Revival architecture, hearkening back to the glorified ancient Athenian democracy, was successful in the new republic, it was said, because it satisfied both the Jacksonians' egalitarian requirements and the Federalists' standards of elegance.

As Americans edged west and prospered, they carried Benjamin's books, spreading his Greek Revival interpretation throughout the Northeast and upper Midwest. Later, Boston architects and builders further influenced domestic design by flinging Italianate, Gothic, Egyptian, and French Empire fancies throughout the Back Bay and the South End. In these two neighborhoods they created the largest and best United States collection of Victorian houses still standing.

During the Victorian period, H. H. Richardson, thought by many to be America's greatest nineteenth-century architect, moved to Boston and designed Trinity Church and heavy stone Romanesque libraries and railroad stations. These piles influenced the design of public buildings in suburban towns all over the East.

When the Colonial Revival movement swept the country in the late 1800s and early 1900s, traditional New England styles spread quickly to places like Winnetka and Palo Alto. Some researchers believe that the Cape Cod house, which continues unabated in popularity for its economy and grace, is the most frequently found house design in the country. English Gothic flowed from Boston to the rest of the country between 1900 and 1940 through the Boston firm of Ralph Adams Cram, who dominated church architecture during that period.

Since World War II, Boston's influence on architecture has come from its universities, as you might expect. Walter Gropius, who left Nazi Germany and came to the Harvard Graduate School of Design in 1937, brought the International Style to the United States. Gropius founded the Bauhaus School in Germany and later the Architects' Collaborative, or TAC, a Cambridge architecture firm of international stature. He and his modernist cohorts—Ludwig Mies van der Rohe and Marcel Breuer, are among the most famous—set the standard in American architecture for thirty years after World War II. Lincoln, a suburb west of Boston, is a showcase for houses designed by this group.

Because of boom times, an inclination for the arts, and three schools of architecture, Boston now has more architects per person than any other American city, the Boston Society of Architects estimates. If one of those architects has a special nationwide influence now, it is probably Benjamin Thompson, whose colorful downtown festival malls, like Boston's Quincy Market—Faneuil Hall Marketplace, if you prefer—are taking over old factories and harbor installations all over the country.

Athens. Boston has been known as the Athens of America since before 1820. The label first likened Boston to the city of Athena, with its dual renown for the arts and learning in one sphere and government in the other. The appellation would have been well understood at that time by all Americans, who, having formed their new democracy, saw themselves as direct ideological descendants of the glorified ancient Athenian and Roman democracies.

Nineteenth-century Boston achieved its classical status partly by following the Puritan habits that valued culture and learning and partly because of maturity. A city that has firmly established government, services, churches, banks, and a thriving economy can devote time and money to endeavors that lift the spirit. Cambridge also enhanced Boston's cultural life. College towns all over America serve up a livelier cultural platter than do noncollege towns.

The intellectual and artistic flowering began shortly after the Revolution. By the mid-1800s, the city's cultural life, its innovations in religion and education, its creation of hospitals, libraries, schools, and other charitable endeavors were unequaled in the United States and in much of Europe, too. Many of the century's most valued writers and thinkers—Hawthorne, Longfellow, Thoreau, Emerson, Holmes—lived in the city and met regularly for dinner and conversation. The *Atlantic Monthly*, the first indigenous American magazine of thought, was begun here. The city became a musical center. The Boston Symphony Orchestra had much to do with that, but so too did an outstanding group of church organists and composers, whose talent and output was unmatched in the rest of the country.

When a son graduated from Harvard, Boston merchant fathers, unlike their counterparts in other cities, did not insist he go into the family business. Among upper-class Bostonians, a life devoted to artistic and intellectual pursuits was commendable, not frivolous.

New York has now surpassed Boston in the arts in sheer numbers of offerings. But with its performances, artists, and institutions, Bostonians enjoy a level of culture matched in no other American city. Culture here is unavoidable; even in the local shopping malls, you are likely to hear a concerto rather than the average Muzak. A recent congressional study showed that companies locate in Boston first for the universities and then for the culture and the arts.

"I must study politics and war that my sons may have liberty to study mathematics and philosophy . . . in order to give their children a right to study painting, poetry, music, architecture, statuary, tapestry and porcelain," wrote John Adams to his wife Abigail in 1780. Bostonians believe that.

Autos. Before you get behind the wheel, consider that you're more likely to have an accident in Massachusetts than you are in any other state in the union. Too many cars, old roads that are too narrow and winding, and poorly designed intersections are only part of the reason. The reason too is the hostile attitude of Boston drivers, who'd rather crash than give way.

Before you get out of your car, consider that in Massachusetts you're twice as likely to have it stolen than in the rest of the nation. It's a mystery why thieves like cars better here than in other places. Once they're behind the wheel, they have to sit in traffic just like everyone else.

Auto theft victims don't have it all bad. Some have been known to feel relief when they realize their car has been stolen: at least they don't have to find a place to park.

Banned in Boston. Certain Irish and Yankee citizens finally found something they could agree on—a distaste for sex. Led by Baptist and Methodist ministers and some puritanical Brahmins, self-appointed guardians of the public morality formed the Watch and Ward Society in the late 1800s. Their intended targets were Boston plays and books. They were only carrying on their forefathers' tradition, among them John Hancock and the otherwise radical Sam Adams, who believed theater to be an evil influence. The Irish Catholic leadership, always more conservative than that of other Catholic nationalities, supported them. City government, through a city censor appointed in 1904, carried out the plan to preserve Bostonians' purity of mind.

You might wonder how such a hostile grip on cultural expression survived in the Athens of America. Perhaps it had to do with Athena's dual nature. The goddess of the useful arts was also a political opportunist. Supporting morality can be politically useful, even if hypocritical. When politics in the city on a hill cooperated with politics in the Emerald Isle, that side of Athena grabbed the power. But Athena's other face did not succumb. Censorship only stepped up Boston's enthusiasm for the arts—theater flourished, music ran rampant, and bookstores sold plenty of books.

The city censor was a confident soul. Who else but one bolstered by a hefty self-righteousness would declare that booksellers could not sell Hemingway or Sin-

15

clair Lewis? Who else but one supported by some of John Winthrop's Puritans and the Catholic Church would have the cheek to order Edward Albee to change lines in *Who's Afraid of Virginia Woolf?* But the decrees were partly ineffectual. When Eugene O'Neill's *Strange Interlude* was banned in Boston in 1929, it simply played in Quincy to overflow crowds.

The last city censor, fittingly named Dick Sinnott, tried to ban *Hair,* not for nudity or obscenity, which probably wouldn't have succeeded in 1970, but for "desecration of the American flag," which may have pulled some support in that time of Vietnam travail. By then, with the Supreme Court breathing down his neck, the city censor was finished in Boston.

Censorship, though, isn't necessarily finished. Now, like everything else in Boston, censorship is a real-estate issue and is controlled by zoning. "Adult entertainment" is restricted to a shrinking area, the Combat Zone, which has been renamed the Midtown Cultural District.

B eans. Baked with molasses or maple syrup, salt pork, and an onion, Boston Baked Beans are the original New England comfort food. Until Boston inhabitants took a wider look at what they ate (see *Julia*), beans and brown bread, including that made by small commercial bakers from the week's unused goods, were a Saturday-night staple. The next morning, fanatic bean lovers or those who refused to cook on Sunday would make from this combination a cold sandwich for breakfast. The common belief is that these recipes came from the Indians.

Boston Baked Beans are now hard to find on menus. They've gone the way of other New England foods like Brown Betty and Boston Cream Pie that are too heavy in a health-conscious era. Chowder is one of the few traditional foods still easy to find. Two places that keep traditional New England foods alive are Durgin Park, the only unrenovated piece of Quincy Market, and the restaurants at the Parker House, that venerable hotel at one of the busiest corners in downtown Boston. The Parker House still serves its famous rolls, 1,308 of them a day baked fresh.

Bells. Every weekday at 8:45 A.M., noon, and 5:00 P.M., the electronic carillon atop the Park Street Church blankets the Common with a concert of favorite hymns. Once again, Park Street Church is showing its knack for bucking more learned trends—a hard row to hoe in learned Boston. The first time was at its founding in 1809, when it established itself as a representative of fire-and-brimstone Congregationalism instead of the more fashionable Unitarianism. Now it bucks more learned tastes in bells. Park Street's bells aren't real, as even a tin ear can tell you. It is a pity, for Boston offers more opportunities to see and hear real bells than any other American city.

The most famous location for real bells is probably Old North Church, where the lanterns signaled to Paul Revere the British route to Lexington and Concord. Old North has a "peal" or tuned set of change-ringing bells, which are rung every Sunday after the 11 o'clock service. Change ringing is a uniquely English tradition in which bell ringers work bell ropes according to mathematical patterns. The more bells, the more possibilities. (As a boy, Paul Revere rang the changes at Old North, or Christ Church, as it was then called.) Of the fifteen sets of change-ringing bells in this country nearly half are in Massachusetts. The best place to watch change ringing is at the Advent Church at the corner of Mt. Vernon and Brimmer every Sunday morning just after 10 o'clock. Advent's bells ring for the *1812 Overture* on the Fourth of July and at the coming of the New Year too.

More bells ring in carillons, played by a person at a keyboard that controls hammers striking stationary

17

bells. Wellesley College and St. Stephen's Church in Cohasset have real carillons. Smaller carillons of fewer than twenty-three bells are called chimes. A chime of eighteen bells is played at the First Church of Christ, Scientist, the "Mother Church," on Huntington Avenue at noon every weekday, on Sundays at about 9:30 A.M., and for the city's major celebrations. Westminster chimes ring there automatically at 8:00 A.M., noon, and 6:00 P.M.

A lone bell clangs every Sunday at ten minutes before eleven in the forever unfinished steeple at King's Chapel. Paul Revere, who, typically for Boston, still draws criticism from bell aficionados for knowing how to cast a bell but not tune it, made and hung this bell in 1772. Revere and his sons and grandsons made almost a thousand bells, many still ringing in New England church towers. A 1926 two-ton English bell, not made by Revere, hangs at Harvard's Memorial Chapel. Its swing can be seen from the Yard. Harvard's other famed bells were purchased after the Russian Revolution from a monastery due for demolition and now ring at Lowell House. The biggest bell in this *zvon* or set weighs thirteen tons and is called Mother Earth.

So much about real bells. Bells, like the Pops, don't have to be the real thing to become a symbol for a city. The Park Street Church carillon, its artificial sound and historical insignificance notwithstanding, is the musical landmark in downtown Boston.

Bestiary. Despite its success in other educational ventures, Boston has never been able to bring about a proper zoo. If you've seen San Diego's, Chicago's, or the Bronx's offerings, you'll never recover from the grim exhibits in Franklin Park or Stoneham. Bostonians have to get their dose of loving animals from the city's sculpture and commercial ventures.

Lions, horses, and eagles grace every city and Boston

is no exception. With British regality, Boston's favorite lion cavorts with a unicorn on top of the eastern Old State House façade. The present representations are copies, because the originals were torn out and burned after the Declaration of Independence was first read there. The city's favorite horses are ridden by Paul Revere in the North End and by General George Washington in the Public Garden. The best eagle sits atop the tall column in the State House parking lot, purportedly representing the original height of Beacon Hill and the location of its colonial beacon.

But the animal icons most revered are a fish, an insect, a family of ducks, and a bevy of swans. If you don't see them in the original, you're likely to see them appropriated by merchants for their own use. For the fish, see *Sacred*. The favored insect is the grasshopper weathervane mounted on Faneuil Hall. This symbol was chosen by Peter Faneuil, it is said, to mimic the weathervane on London's Royal Exchange. When Deacon Shem Downe made it in 1742, he reportedly used glass doorknobs for eyes. The ducks (see *Ducklings*) are the bronze Mrs. Mallard and her eight little ones who strut beside a path in the Public Garden, headed toward the pond. Children are permitted to touch, straddle, converse with, and otherwise engage these renditions of Robert McCloskey's heroes and heroines in *Make Way for Ducklings*. The century-old swans glide on boats around the Public Garden pond from mid-April through September, enfolding the young men and women who pedal the boats.

Black-crowned Night Herons. Black and white birds, two feet tall with extended beaks, trailing long feathers from their crowns. They perch awkwardly in trees or wade along the Charles River shore looking every bit like small penguins who have lost their polish. They spend the day along the Esplanade, roost at the dam by Watertown Square, and nest on the Harbor Islands.

Common bird life in Boston is more varied than you might expect. The usual gulls, house sparrows, pigeons, blue jays, robins, mockingbirds, and crows pick around for fish, insects, or crumbs tossed by crowds. Downtown neighborhoods, parks, and waterways are also home to mallards, cormorants, cardinals, house finches, nighthawks, nuthatches, chickadees, titmice, downy and hairy woodpeckers, and song sparrows. Warblers, white-throated sparrows, red-wing blackbirds, and pine siskins stop by downtown green spaces on their migrations.

At least one red-tailed hawk resides on Boston Common. After he catches a squirrel, pigeon, or rat, he sometimes attracts a crowd by eating it in plain view. Massachusetts' largest population of snowy owls winters on the outer runways at the airport. Another winter spectacle are the thousands of starlings roosting under the bridge where Interstate 93 and Route 1 (on maps sometimes designated Interstate 95) split going north. Boston's Arnold Arboretum and Mount Auburn Cemetery in Cambridge play host in May to thousands of migrating warblers. East Boston's Belle Isle Marsh at Orient Heights is a favorite with birders all year long.

Downtown high-rises provide the local peregrine falcon population, numbering, in usual circumstances, one pair and their chicks, with simulated cliffs. The peregrines were brought back into Boston in 1984 by the Massachusetts Division of Fish and Wildlife. They prey on other high-flying birds and build nests on business executives' window ledges thirty floors up. Their hold on their experimental habitat is still tenuous: only a few falcon pairs have laid eggs here. Only one pair has successfully raised chicks to maturity. Peregrines are the fastest bird in the world, diving at more than 180 miles an hour. In crowded spaces, they stay high to catch their food. Workers in local office towers have sometimes been treated to the spectacle of a falcon dive bombing for prey past their windows.

Blue Laws. These Puritan remnants, forbidding certain Sunday and holiday activities, were written on blue paper, say some. Others contend they were called the *bloody* laws, as well as the *black and blue* laws, fairly describing the punishment that would be meted out for breaking them. The chastisement now threatens to savage the pocketbook instead of the body, but we've still got them, albeit in faded form. Support for doing away with these laws completely is minimal. People here still like to feel they've got what the Commonwealth calls *a common day of rest.* You can now expect department and grocery stores to be open on Sundays from noon until six. But most smaller shops are closed. You may be able to buy a car. You can buy a beer over the counter, but not at a package store. If you're coming from a state where you can pick up drinks for a weekend party on the spur of the moment, the blue laws can leave you dry: In Massachusetts, you have to plan ahead.

Bookstores. When Boston's intelligentsia get entrepreneurial, they either go high-tech or open a bookstore. Boston's Yellow Pages list almost 300 bookstores, or about one for every 2,500 souls. No one ever has to suffer with nothing but bestsellers or romances. Bookstores are the reason many Bostonians could never move.

Boston has a bookstore for every purpose. The Brattle Bookstore on West Street offers old books. Goodspeed's on Beacon Street sells old prints as well. The Harvard Coop (rhymes with *loop*) in Cambridge and the B.U. Bookstore vie for the title as biggest and having most books. Kate's Mystery Books—well, you can guess. (Kate's, by the way, was once demolished by an MBTA bus that struck the side of her North Cambridge store.) One bookstore—the Harvard Book Store Cafe on Newbury Street—is also a restaurant. Schoenhof's in Harvard Square sells only foreign books. The Globe

Corner Bookstore in downtown Boston specializes in travel. Discount bookstores, occult bookstores, quiet little reading-room bookstores, exchange bookstores, feminist bookstores, gay bookstores, even run-of-the-mill national chain bookstores—they're all here. All these bookstores foster book clubs. Beacon Hill alone has at least four. In Cambridge, the number is infinite. Some are for couples, some for men, others for women. Some combine dinner with discussion.

In a book-crazed place like Boston, it is fitting that someone should have invented a computerized reading machine, blending the two most popular entrepreneurial ventures. Ray Kurzweil, M.I.T. whiz, fiddled around with sounds and electronics and formed a company to produce the Kurzweil Reading Machine. This electronic Bill Cavness reads aloud from any book under its scanner. (Mr. Cavness is the star of *Reading Aloud,* which originates in Boston on WGBH public radio.) Mr. Kurzweil has retired to invent more amazing electronics, and the Kurzweil Company is now a part of Xerox.

Brahmins. Boston's aristocracy, descended from nineteenth-century sea captains, ship owners, railroad builders, and mill founders, are known by this Asian-sounding label. Oliver Wendell Holmes coined it in 1860, referring to a kind of upper-class Bostonian who lived an intellectual and cultured life of relative simplicity, more in tune, they believed, with Indian ascetics than with the wealthy in other American cities. Brahmins lived in the Back Bay or on Beacon Hill, intermarried shamelessly, voted Republican, and ran everything in Boston. They lived, dressed, and spent money modestly. They read the *Boston Evening Transcript,* bought their food at S. S. Pierce, and shopped at R. H. Stearns. At their worst they were mean-spirited, arrogant, exclusionary, and small-minded—in other words, no different from most other people. At their best they were imaginative, curious,

22

indefatigable, and astonishingly productive. Their far-reaching business enterprises, their literary output, their scientific discoveries, and their ideas influenced every facet of American life.

The life they promoted—productivity, intellect, and ease tempered with self-denial—remains the standard by which contemporary Bostonians of all stripes measure success, but it naturally couldn't last in its original vigor. The Brahmins dispersed into the suburbs— Brookline, Dover, Dedham, and the North Shore. The Irish took over city politics. The *Transcript,* S. S. Pierce, and Stearns folded. People who bragged about making money and spending it took over the Republican Party. So a good number of Brahmins had to defect to the Democrats, who had begun to extol goo-goo (good government) policies that sounded suspiciously like those claimed by the Brahmins' Puritan antecedents. The Brahmins' hold on financial institutions and law firms lasted longer, but even at the institutions formerly pure Yankee the newcomers now are of all origins.

Brahmins still live, most of them with blood less blue and trust funds less trusty. If you come upon a man or woman with a name something like Coolidge Faneuil Saltonstall, you'll know you've found one.

Breakdown Lane.   The driving lane to choose when the traffic creeps. It's a good place to relieve boredom and test reflexes. Think of the thrill, skimming the pavement on the far right while all those saps in the legal lanes are backed up for miles. We all have to get home from the Cape to the best of our ability and in Boston if you don't seize the opportunity to beat out your fellow man and woman, somebody else will. When the traffic is moving well you can still enjoy the sport. Be careful to whip back into the bumper-to-bumper traffic on your left should a real breakdown loom ahead.

The most popular highway for breakdown-lane driving is Route 3, between Boston and the Cape. The Mass. Pike is also a prime spot, especially in early September when students return to college. Route 93 North suffers from breakdown-lane travel on the "blessing of the motorcycles" weekend in New Hampshire. The state police don't seem to get aroused when they observe this practice, so no one ever gets arrested. Other drivers, however, are not amused. Some straddle the right-hand solid line so as to block breakdown-lane drivers, inciting horn honking, bumper brushing, and macho maneuvering. The Mass. DPW (Department of Public Works) finally succumbed to tradition on Route 3 and made breakdown-lane driving legal on the northernmost leg between Braintree and Boston. Warning: Do not break down.

Brew. Despite our reputation for puritanical ways, New Englanders have always been renowned for drinking. At 3.33 cases per year in Massachusetts, we consume more alcohol per adult than the rest of the country. Other New England states lag but little behind.

Bostonians come by their taste for brew as they do for other pleasures—historically. In the late 1600s the Puritans produced rum at about a dozen distilleries. The colonists were also fond of madeira and other European wines and of country cider. Bostonians and their neighbors ran an efficient trade route importing molasses from the West Indies, making it into rum in New England, and shipping the rum to Africa, where they traded it for slaves. When New Englanders began to feel contrition for their early ways, they became abolitionists. Some abolitionists were also in the temperance movement, once again combining rum and slaves.

Bricks. The downtown Bostonian's favored building material and, since protected historical districts were set aside, of necessity. They're everywhere, used for the sidewalks, as structural walls in houses and office buildings, and exposed on interior walls. In some eras, the bricks were painted. Now it is fashionable to keep them in their natural state, making Boston a red city. Old records show that brick was so desirable in the colonial period, it was sometimes imported from Holland. Why do we see so much of it when wood was so plentiful? Probably because brick was fashionable in Georgian England. When prosperous colonial merchants built their homes and offices, they wanted to keep up in style with the Mother Country. Bulfinch, the architect who so gracefully transferred English style to this part of world, was a great fan. Workmen newly arrived from England were experienced in making and working with it. Brick also helped prevent fires, the scourge of colonial Boston.

With so much brick around, Bostonians have grown to appreciate its subtleties. Most downtown residents will readily, if asked, flaunt their knowledge about Flemish bond, in which the bricks are laid alternately with first end out and then side out in each row. They know English bond, in which the bricklayer alternates a row of bricks set with ends out with a row set with sides out. Most people can easily envision common bond, laid with all bricks side out in staggered rows.

Bulfinch. The Christopher Wren of Boston. This late eighteenth-century and early nineteenth-century architect is responsible for much of Boston's appearance today. He built in brick and granite and emulated elegant English styles. He designed the Massachusetts State House, Massachusetts

Hall at Harvard, the North End church now known as St. Stephen's, part of Mass General, and several private houses on or near Beacon Hill. He added to and embellished Faneuil Hall. Later architects imitated him. Some of the nineteenth-century granite wharves now transformed into condominiums are among newer buildings influenced by the Bulfinch style. Bulfinch served as chairman of the Boston board of selectmen from 1797 to 1818, a time of energetic building in the city. He later served as architect for the Capitol in Washington.

Bulfinch was more than an architect. His talent for the specialty we now call urban planning started Boston on the road to planned developments set in a grid relieved by small green ovals. Louisburg (pronounced Lewisburg) Square and the small green spaces dotting the South End are prime examples. The proverbial Boston cowpaths were only in the colonial part of the city.

Just because Boston has the same grids as any other red-blooded American city, don't expect streets to line up with one another. When a new section in the mud flats was filled, planners would lay out the new streets, not bothering to align them with older sections. This crazy quilt of grids forms the pattern of the city outside the colonial section.

Burying Grounds. No other American city has as many downtown cemeteries as Boston. These pockets of greenery provide unexpected relief from the bricks and asphalt. The old graves have been disturbed from time to time as the city has grown up around them. Some graves hold more than one body, some have none. Headstones have been rearranged so that no one can be sure that the person named is the one who lies underneath. The burying grounds make for macabre digging when utility lines or subway tunnels are excavated. Workmen are likely to find old skeletons in unmarked graves beyond the present boundaries. Theoretically, if you are the descendant of someone whose body occupies a tomb, if you hold title to the tomb, and if the tomb has room, the powers that be in the Parks and Recreation Department will allow you to be buried there. Practically, it almost never happens. The last person to be buried in one of the downtown burying grounds was a descendant of John Winthrop, inserted into his tomb in the mid-1980s.

C **entral Artery.** The real name of the road through the city that maps call the Fitzgerald Expressway, Route 3, or Interstate 93. Some refer to it as "the world's longest parking lot." Traffic is stopped dead on the road much of the day, and fourteen-hour jams are predicted for the 1990s. The Artery also takes the prize as the Interstate system's most accident-filled stretch.

This elevated superhighway was built in the 1950s, when we didn't yet know there were limits to the good the automobile could do. We razed lots of buildings and then raised a mile-and-a-half road through downtown Boston that is about as appealing as a gash on a face. It's now to go underground at a cost of a few billion. One congressman, upon hearing that the state planned to bury the Central Artery, commented that it would be cheaper to raise the city, which might also take less time.

Despite official predictions for a completed road before the twentieth century ends, most Bostonians will tell you they won't see it in their lifetime. Considering how much the construction disrupts parking, stops traffic, and spreads debris over the financial district, the complaints are relatively few. We're so used to traffic, parking, and trash problems in downtown Boston that we barely notice a modest increase.

When the road is completely underground, Boston will have a windfall that only a pinched little city can appreciate: twenty-two acres of prime-location, vacant land above the buried road. In the meantime, this massive public works project will keep the Boston economy rolling for another decade, at least.

Change. A true Bostonian prefers things as they are and regards change with suspicion. "Although it may not be exciting, very often the success of an organization is marked by an absence of change," said a recent president of the Beacon Hill Civic Association speaking to that group's board of directors. Everyone nodded in complete agreement.

Chaos. If you live here, you get used to it. Unexplained events, illogical decisions, no decisions—you just accept the mess because the city seems to survive in spite of total chaos. The driving is, of course, legendary, but it is only a symbol for deeper waters. Do you really care if the street signs are wrong? You'll either get lost or eventually find out where you're going. Does it really matter that one week after the city paves your street for the first time in thirty-one years, the cable television people dig a trench in it to lay their cable? You could ask yourself, "Don't they coordinate these things?" But questions like that will only frustrate you and won't improve the condition. Why is it that Boston is the last place on the continent to get cable television, anyway?

For years, people didn't bother to pay state taxes or parking tickets, because government officials didn't bother to collect them. For years, until pressed hard by public opinion, the police refused to patrol on foot. Were the streets too dangerous for them or had they, unlike any other true Bostonian, grown to like their cars? A superintendent of schools, whose job it is to keep the schools safe, had to send his child to a suburban school system to protect her from gangs that had made her a target. Everyone sympathized with the school superintendent. Things just don't make sense here. The most amazing thing is that it doesn't make any difference.

Chat. *The Boston Globe*'s Confidential Chat, begun in 1884, is the oldest newspaper column in the country devoted to "housekeeping" topics. Since 1922, the column has consisted of anonymous letters asking for advice, recipes, or support in time of trouble as well as answers, also anonymous, from other readers to questions earlier writers asked. The letter writers take names like *Carpenter's Mom* or *Olive A. Sudden*. The most dramatic requests seek advice on problems involving children, spouses, and in-laws and their rotten ways. The answers may scold or praise, sympathize or criticize. This column waxes and wanes in size and frequency depending on the editor and cultural forces, but over the years it has been one of the small voices straining against the fragmentation that characterizes this city.

The *Globe* doesn't spend all, or even much of its time on household matters. It is the city's newspaper of record. Its fat sections cover the news extensively, although the prevailing wisdom has it that the *Boston Herald,* the *Globe*'s tabloid competition, usually scoops it on State House and City Hall news. The *Globe* used to have a lot of competition. In the late 1800s, Boston had at least nine daily newspapers. Now only three are left, including the *Christian Science Monitor,* which is aimed at more of a national audience than the other two dailies. One of the *Globe*'s biggest competitors now is the *New York Times,* which covers Boston news cursorily, but regularly. The innumerable small and sassy weeklies also capture much of the newspaper reading public.

One of the *Globe*'s most popular political cartoonists is Paul Szep. Mr. Szep has a grown-up daughter, Amy. If you look carefully, you can find her name in his drawings.

Cheers. The question tourists continue to ask most is "Where is Cheers?" Let's get it out of the way: under 84 Beacon Street, across from the Public Garden, where it goes by the name Bull and Finch Pub. (Bulfinch, get it?) You'll recognize it by the line outside the door and the sound of cameras clicking.

It's fitting that a television show has been made about a Boston pub because the city has lots of good ones—a leftover, perhaps, from a British past bolstered by Irish preferences. City Hall types hang out at the Marshall House, the Purple Rose, and The Exchange, all within a block behind City Hall. Architects clog the Harvest Restaurant's bar in Harvard Square. State politicians go to The Last Hurrah at the Parker House. Kennedy School students go to Charlie's. Writers officially hang out at Tapas in Cambridge at least one Wednesday each month. Amrheins Restaurant in South Boston, though not technically a bar, is a favorite hangout for both Southie business types and politicians. Bell ringers go to the Commonwealth Brewery on Tuesday nights. Those who are over the hill or don't know where else to go, go to the Ritz.

Neighborhood bars, like everything else about Boston neighborhoods, can sometimes inspire turf feelings. Notable exceptions are Doyle's in Jamaica Plain, which attracts JP's melange of residents—working people and yuppies, blacks and whites—and serves some of the best hearty beers in town. The Sevens on Charles Street on Beacon Hill, where neighborhood people go when the Bull and Finch gets too crowded, is also inclusive. An unexplained phenomenon is the Phoenix Room. Its Mexican food is second-rate and its location out on Commonwealth Avenue is far from downtown, but almost anyone who has lived here more than a few years has been there.

C **ondos.** Condominiums are nothing new. But Boston specializes: How about a small abode for your automobile? The top models go for as high as $500 a square foot. That's not bad for a rectangle of concrete that after a few cars have leaked oil on it probably qualifies as a hazardous waste site. When the first parking condominiums went up for sale in the 1970s a block from the Public Garden, cynics scoffed at the high price—about $10,000. After a little more than a decade the price has increased tenfold. Skip office buildings, apartments, and raw land. There's a limit to what people will pay for those. But people will pay anything for a parking place. It's the best real estate investment in downtown Boston.

C **onstruction.** After browsing in bookstores, Boston's most popular pastime is watching construction. At any one time, at least a quarter of the city seems to be undergoing building for a new subway line or office building, depression of a roadway, or conversion of an old warehouse into housing.

Construction is loud and dirty. So is Boston. Construction debris covers up Boston's daily debris and nobody has to clean up. What a relief to us all.

C **ontradictions.** Back Bay is not a bay. Beacon Hill has no beacon. South Cove is no cove. Be wary of signs pointing you toward an expressway. It usually means you'll get on a slow road. Despite the street sign, there's no Scollay Square. Only five people were killed in the Boston Massacre. In this most walkable of cities, pedestrians have trouble getting across the street. South Boston is not the south part of Boston. East Boston is north. Cape Cod is an island. According to maps, the Upper Cape is really the lower part, and the Lower Cape is the upper extension. The medical capital of the world is also the headquarters of

Christian Science, which rejects the doctor's powers in favor of God's. Maine may be north but to get there we go down east. Cape Cod houses did not originate on the Cape, although plenty stand there. The Harvard Bridge goes to M.I.T. In Boston, an avenue is most likely to be a tiny alley. Boston Cream Pie is a cake. Boston is not the hub of the universe, but a regional city in a small corner of the country with more than its share of charm.

Copper. The state bird is the chickadee. The city metal ought to be copper. The best kind is no shiny new penny, but the verdigris on a long-ago installation. Copper adorns rooftops, trims architectural features, and its weathered green is copied in paint on some bridges and lampposts. The Charles Street MBTA Station is entirely fashioned in the material. Copper originally covered the State House dome, installed by that man who had his hand in every pie, Paul Revere.

Crowds. The cannons boom over the river, the bells of Advent Church peal in jubilation, fireworks streak the sky. Boston may be the only city in America where inhabitants return from vacations so that they can enjoy a hot city on the Fourth of July.

Because traffic makes the roads impassable, most of the 250,000 plus enthusiasts walk, paddle down the river, or take the Red Line, running on a beefed-up schedule for the occasion. They stake out their claim to a piece of the Esplanade with a blanket early in the day. Those who live close send relief squads.

The day passes. The crowd grows, finally stretching from the Hatch Shell past the Harvard Bridge. Boats, canoes, pontoons, and crew shells bob in the estuary. The Pops warms up with "The Star-Spangled Banner" and Sousa marches. It's all a prelude to the main attraction. The *1812 Overture* is not the national anthem, but it ought to be, judging by the verve with which the musicians attack it and the tingles in the spines of the crowd.

The Fourth of July is the perfect city celebration. It is stirring, safe, full of humor and entertainment, and without hassle. Everyone is welcome. Everyone behaves well.

The citywide jubilation on the Fourth is matched only by First Night, held inside and outside, no matter what the weather on New Year's Eve, and Patriot's Day, celebrated on the Monday closest to April 18 with the Boston Marathon. In all these events, Boston Proper throbs with festivities, spirits are high, everyone comes. These are family holidays and the city is the family, with everyone—all ages and ethnic backgrounds— welcome and having a fine time. Because the streets are clogged with pedestrians, no one ever comes by car. Let that be fair warning.

Curley. Mayor, governor, congressman, jailbird, James Michael Curley is the standard by which political corruption and cachet are measured in Massachusetts. Not that the Commonwealth has a corner on the market in sleaze, but it has a history of canonizing crooked public officials who, by ingenuity or flamboyance, were thought to have confounded the Yankee stranglehold on power in Boston. The problem was that the tradition lasted long after the Yankees had conceded. The problem for Curley was that with all his shenanigans, he still did not die a rich man.

Schooled in the old Irish ward politics, Curley ran and won his first campaign (for alderman) in 1905 from jail. Later, as mayor, he looked out for the poor and the powerless. His charm and shrewdness and his followers' devotion returned him to office repeatedly.

34

He didn't always win. In defeat, he played to the audience. To steal thunder from the governor who replaced him, he announced his engagement to his second wife on his opponent's inaugural day. He spent part of his fourth and last term as mayor in 1947 in a federal penitentiary for fraud.

With an irony that makes history worth it, Curley was done in not by the Yankees but by another Irishman. When the rest of the Massachusetts congressional delegation pressured Truman to commute the aging Curley's sentence, U.S. Congressman John Fitzgerald Kennedy refused to go along. Some accuse Kennedy of ingratitude, for it was Curley's 1945 run for mayor that opened up the old man's congressional seat to the young war hero. Some say Kennedy was merely settling accounts with Curley, who had defeated JFK's grandfather, Honey Fitz, for mayor in 1913. No matter what Kennedy's motive, his action was the signal that the old ward skulduggery was losing its savor and that the no less vivid Kennedy style would now hold sway.

Politics changed in Massachusetts, but Curley manages to live on in myth, music, book, and bronze. Songwriter Frank Hatch, father of the erstwhile gubernatorial candidate, reminded us to "vote early and often for Curley." Edwin O'Connor based the *The Last Hurrah* upon the mayor, making it harder to tell where truth ends and fiction begins. One statue was not enough to memorialize this larger-than-life man: two Curley likenesses sit and stand in Dock Square beneath City Hall, extending a hand to present-day constituents.

D **ark Days.** Dark Days were an eighteenth-century New England phenomenon that may have been the closest example in the region's history to conditions in an apocalyptic nuclear winter. On Dark Days the sun rose but no one could see it. The chickens stayed on their roosts. The sky remained dark all day. Historians theorize that Dark Days were caused by ash and smoke carried by wind currents from vast forest fires in the Great Lakes wilderness. Dark Days continued intermittently until the mid-nineteenth century.

D **ebris and Dirt.** Visitors and some residents claim that Boston's streets are disgusting. Piles of dog droppings. Trash. Grit and grime. Weeds. Pieces of unidentifiable objects. Broken sidewalks. Abandoned cars. They compare it to New York, which at least has the relief of well cared-for streets on the Upper East Side. They say if Cairo, with 14 million people and few resources, can pick up, why can't Boston?

But dirt is a quaint Boston tradition. We shed the Empire's cleanliness along with the Empire's godliness at the Revolution and took on debris and Unitarianism instead. It's been this way for so long that now we'd feel uneasy if we became tidy. Besides, if we spent all that time cleaning, how would we ever get to Symphony or the Red Sox?

Clean streets don't fit in with our other customs. Why should we provide trash barrels when we're not organized enough to empty them? How can we fine errant dog owners when we don't bother to stop drivers for running red lights? It's our habit to throw candy wrappers and what-have-you on the sidewalk. It's traditional for Boston dog owners to pay no attention to their neighbor's discomfort at the smells they leave behind. Residents long ago gave up on their own sidewalks because the neighbors' trash will soon blow into any place they clean up. Why should city officials spend municipal money on a decadent frill like street sweeping? Their task is to make policy, not clean up.

Decline. Decline saved Boston. We could have been Atlanta. We could have been Detroit. But we were in such desperate straits that we couldn't imagine who would move into new buildings if we bulldozed the old ones and started over. Except for a couple of major mistakes, we didn't. And now, as other cities find themselves one vast shopping mall and suburb, Boston is a bona fide city. People come here and say Boston looks European. It does. But with its neighborhood centers and walkable streets, it's more like America—the way it used to be.

Boston was the largest city in British North America until the mid-eighteenth century. Even when Philadelphia and New York overtook it in population, Boston's economy continued to grow vigorously with shipping, manufacturing, and banking. But after the Civil War, the tide of Boston's fortunes turned. New York became the great East Coast port as well as the nation's banking and financial center. Boston businessmen continued to run a few national companies. The city's manufacturing and banking sectors held on for a while. But Boston slipped into permanent status as a regional capital.

The twentieth century speeded the decline of the city's fortunes. The shoe and textile industries died.

Except for a temporary flurry during World War II, harbor activity quieted. The city's population plummeted from a high in 1950 of more than 800,000 to about 560,000 in 1980.

When the technology and service-based economy turned things around in the 1980s, Bostonians hardly knew how to act. The inhabitants here don't like change. We believe in the past as much as the future. Prosperity brings problems. There must be more to life than geometrically multiplying traffic snarls, constant architectural squabbles, inadequate public transportation, and costly demands to expand the sewers and water lines. Most of us long perversely for the good old days when all we had to worry about was explaining why leaves change color in the fall.

Developer. The work all Boston politicians aspire to when they leave public office. Like everything else Bostonians hold dear, developers have a long history in this city. Beacon Hill is an early product of developers, one of whom was the architect Charles Bulfinch. He eventually spent time in jail for bankruptcy when one of his projects didn't pan out. Back Bay and the South End also are the developers' legacy: they would build a few row houses and sell them off. Developers have left Boston with layers of architecture, representing every era since the founding of the country.

Doggerel. No melody chimes in the word Massachusetts. Can you imagine "Massachusetts, Here I Come"? The name Boston, with no romantic image, is a dud. How would it sound: "I Left My Heart in Boston"? The city has spawned only a few memorable lines: Longfellow's "Midnight Ride of Paul Revere," Frank Hatch Sr.'s song about the "Old Howard," and the tale made famous by the Kingston

Trio about Charlie's never-ending ride on the old MTA. Bostonians have had to make do with a few little verses:

This is good old Boston
The home of the bean and the cod,
Where the Lowells speak only to Cabots
And the Cabots speak only to God.

To confirm what you already know about the weather by looking at the signal atop the Old John Hancock Building in Back Bay:

Steady blue, clear view.
Flashing blue, clouds are due.
Steady red, rain ahead.
Flashing red, snow instead.
(Flashing red in the summer means the Red Sox game has been canceled.)

One version of a ditty for bouncing little children on the knee:

Trot, trot to Boston,
Trot, trot to Lynn.
Careful, little baby,
Don't fall in.

Ducklings. The ducklings, near the corner of Beacon and Charles streets, head toward the pond in the Public Garden. These statues belie the conventional wisdom that Boston only takes to heart anything more than a hundred years old. Is it because this one is designed for children?

Despite dirt, traffic, and questionable public schools, downtown Boston is a fine place for children to grow up in. Early in the morning children crowd the Frog Pond and the Esplanade swimming pool. Then they might take a foray into the playgrounds on the Common or in the North End. Little ones head to the Public

Garden to ride the Swan Boats, pat the bronze ducklings, or climb the trees. (Surely this exercise is forbidden, but every Boston child does it anyway.) Before heading home, they might make an excursion to Jack's Joke Shop for powdery pretend cigarettes on which a child can puff—a sure way to startle health-conscious passers-by. Another day might hold a trip to the Children's Museum, roller skating on the Esplanade, or a whale watch.

Children can run their own activities at a fairly early age in Boston because they city is small and the pedestrian quality makes it reasonably safe. Youngsters master the subways and get acquainted with neighborhood shopkeepers early in their lives.

Teenagers have the best time in Boston Proper. The fun costs little and city kids don't get that glazed look that comes from hanging out too much in malls. Kids sail down streets on skateboards. They sail in another style on the Charles River, learning and hanging around the boats for $1 a summer. They get together in the evening at the free concerts on the Esplanade. They take the commuter rail or the subway to the beach. They congregate in Harvard Square with Cambridge teenagers. Suburban kids also come in to the Square to participate in a little urban sophistication. In winter, Boston kids skate on the bumpy Public Garden Pond and at the MDC rinks, or ski and sled on the Common. They go to the museums and performances as much as adults do. They work after school and during summers because jobs are plentiful downtown.

The duckling statues, set down in 1987, are a tribute to Robert McCloskey, author of *Make Way for Ducklings,* which, drawn from a child's-eye view, recognizes that children find Boston welcoming. This is one of the few North American cities that can make the claim.

E **ffluent.** Every New Year's Day for almost
ninety years the L Street Brownies have run
across the beach at the L Street Bathhouse in
South Boston and thrown themselves into Boston Harbor for a refreshing swim. All Bostonians would join
them if it weren't for one problem: the water is too
polluted.

You'd think a little dirt wouldn't dissuade an inhabitant of the litter capital of the world from enjoying the
brisk January waters of the North Atlantic. But our tolerance has its limits. Boston Harbor being the dirtiest in
the nation, we've decided to clean it up to the tune of
more than $6 billion. The cities and towns around the
harbor grudgingly agreed to a cleanup because a judge
threatened to close down the commercial real-estate
market if we didn't.

Sewage problems are a part of our tradition. Boston
has always used the harbor and rivers as communal
privies and dumping grounds. But what goes out sometimes comes back in with the tide. We had to fix some
of the problems. We filled in the Back Bay partly because the stink from backed-up sewage was so intense.
Bay Village had a number of sewage disasters, so
nineteenth-century engineers raised 200 buildings and
several streets in that neighborhood to new foundations
more than fourteen feet above the old ones. After these
feats, accomplished by horses and men, pushing a tunnel more than ten miles out into the ocean and building
two new treatment plants, as we are doing in the
present Boston Harbor cleanup, is a piece of cake.

41

The harbor clean-up will be accomplished in typical Boston style. Home water and sewer bills are expected to reach $1,000 annually by the end of the 1990s, bolstering Boston's reputation as one of the most costly cities in the Western Hemisphere. We'll contribute to history by presenting to the Smithsonian a sewage system artifact, a still-functioning steam engine from the East Boston Pumping Station, when it is removed from service. And this project will continue our prosperity, employing almost 2,000 workers right at the same time as that other massive public works project, the Central Artery and third harbor tunnel dig. How can it miss?

Emerald Necklace. Our grandiose name for a grandiose design—almost 2,200 acres of city-owned parkland running from the Common through the hinterlands. The parks needed a designer name because we engaged the Yves St. Laurent of nineteenth century landscape architects to get it going. One of Frederick Law Olmsted's other projects was New York's Central Park. Only in print do we use "emerald necklace." In conversation we usually disregard the metaphor and call our green space "parks." Not everyone supported creating these parks. Some of our forebears believed offering the unwashed masses their own local garden of Eden would increase public immorality. Luckily the forces of Eden carried the day.

We managed to build most of the Emerald Necklace. Then we ran into our old nemesis—cleaning up: we didn't. The parks complemented the streets of Boston in excessive accumulations of trash and no repairs. At last count we were spending about $17 per person on park maintenance. The city to which we are most compared in appeal, San Francisco, was spending $75 per person. Funding for improved maintenance has been promised, and several groups have sprung up to support the parks. Expectations run low.

England. Some Bostonians like to believe that Boston is just like an English city. This is a fine point of view if we're talking to other Americans. But why should a Londoner come to Boston if he thinks he's getting what he just left? Let's put things straight. Boston is not like England. It finally has better food, for one thing. It also has better medical help and hotels, a closer airport, and more ice cream. It has fewer Englishmen and women, for only 8 percent of Boston's citizens consider themselves of English descent. It has fewer theater offerings than London, although it's the best in the States outside of New York. It has poorer public transportation than London, unrecognizable taxis, and the only royals are Kennedys.

All you Englishmen and women, if you want to ease into America, we can offer you its essence, Boston style. We will treat you to the best basketball, baseball, hospitals, universities, ice cream, and hard liquor. We don't promise to be friendly; we're more likely to be rude. We'll offer quaint Americanisms like the worst water pollution and serious venture capital. You won't feel at home. You'll love it.

Expensive. The reason we're so bad-tempered is that it costs so damn much to live in the Athens of America. Food, clothing, and incidentals are regularly the highest-priced in the nation. Boston, at almost $250 a day, is second only to New York in business travelers' expenses. A house or a condominium will set the average buyer back at least $200,000—placing Boston housing costs regularly among the four highest in the U.S.A. We are more likely to send our children, including college students, to private schools. We have to pay for more parking tickets than the usual urban dweller. Our insurance costs are among the highest because our cars get stolen more often than elsewhere. Water and sewer costs are rising and are predicted to be the highest in the nation by the end of the century. We don't care that personal income in Massachusetts grew faster than in any other state during the 1980s and we ought to be able to afford these extras. We'd prefer to complain.

F **all.** The Color is not the only reason New Englanders enjoy the fall. Unless a hurricane passes through, September and October promise fewer days of rain than other months. Upcountry is beautiful, but so too are the Cape and the Islands at this time of year, when most tourists have gone home. Summer and the Gulf Stream have warmed the North Atlantic. Warmth is relative, of course. The story is that New England fishermen don't bother to learn to swim because they won't survive in the cold water long enough to be saved.

Fall is best because the other seasons are not what they're cracked up to be. Winters are disappointing if you like weather. We have less snow than Milwaukee, Cleveland, Pittsburgh, and Hartford. Snow is a perfect excuse for not getting to work on time and not going to school at all. You'd think summer in a northern city would be nice and cool. Sometimes it is. In 1816 every month of the summer saw frosts and the rye didn't ripen. Usually, however, we suffer some 90 degree days and, though it is cooler than Washington or Baltimore, Boston, on the average, is more humid. We don't have as much sunshine as Denver, but we have more than Houston. We don't have spring. Winter has a habit of lingering until May, when a snow filled nor'easter can still attack. Then it gets hot.

Now the answer to the second most common question in Boston. (See *Cheers*.) The trees change color in the fall because the shrinking daylight and cooling temperatures trigger the tree to stop manufacturing green chlorophylls, which provide food for the tree. As the tree uses up the chlorophylls, other colors that were masked by the green pigments or made in shutting down food intake, appear. Trees change color all over the world, but the New England show is one of the best. The cool, bright days and chilly nights intensify the color. The typical New England mixture of trees— sugar maples, oak, birch, ash, and evergreens—offers optimal variation. The rolling hills expose more trees to view than do flat terrains.

F **ens.** A marsh in England. Our Fens lies behind the Museum of Fine Arts and Northeastern University, between the Isabella Stewart Gardner Museum and Fenway Park. Formerly tidal flats, the land progressively became drier as the Back Bay was filled and the Charles River dammed. The adjoining uplands hold the Victory Gardens. The lowlands have been taken over by tall, feathery phragmites, which obscure a very urban collection of trash. Although the police deny it, a rumor persists that after summer passes the drying reeds produce a dead body or two. Also rumored because of the obvious evidence is that the Fenway reeds provide cover for lovers. It's probably not the safest one. The Fens gave its name to the Fenway and subsequently Fenway Park.

F **ilene's Automatic Bargain Basement.** All over New England the underground part of a building is called the cellar. When you hear the word "basement" there's no question what the speaker is referring to. The Basement is the legendary lower two floors in Filene's, a fine department store, much like department stores anywhere. But the Basement is like no other place, not even its clones at newer suburban locations. The subterranean decoration is pure pre-World War II, necessary for creating the right ambiance. The prices are good from the beginning and they get better after the two "scheduled markdowns." The high quality of much merchandise there and the pricing policy are the reasons miserly Bostonians sometimes wear haute couture or a well-tailored suit.

We speak of "hitting the Basement." Special sale days involving Saks, Neiman Marcus, Brooks Brothers, or Bergdorf's are treated more like festivals than shopping sprees. Families are consulted. Some groups send a representative. On those days it's best to arrive early at Washington Station via subway—either the Red or the Orange line will get you there—and wait in line at the Basement entrance until it opens, usually at 9:30, but on these special days, sometimes at 8:00 A.M. At this hour, the merchandise is in as good an order as you'll find it anytime. Some Basement specialists consider it unsporting to hit the Basement when the place is orderly. If they haven't discovered the only $99 Karl Lagerfeld raincoat in America lurking in the sweater bin, their victory has been too easy.

The most successful Basement shoppers have an open mind about what they're looking for. They may also have the inside track, for clerks have been known to slip favored customers information about special offerings in advance. Only the men trying on suits get dressing rooms; women must wear something they can easily take off or hike up. The method is to run for the nearest rack and fight over the clothes, scrutinizing the fabric and the cut for evidence that the garment is something that people in Houston are buying in salons for several thousand dollars. We check for rips or missing belts, although we may not insist that a garment be whole or even clean. We keep our own belongings and the merchandise we are considering clutched to our chests. We wear what we buy, sometimes for years. "I found it in the Basement," is considered the only shopping conversation permissible among Boston's well-bred.

Everyone's heard the stories. How women in their slips slug it out over little Yves St. Laurents. How the men prowl the aisles to leer. How society matrons, lawyers, and grocery clerks jostle one another around the same bin of shoes. How some shoppers have been known to stuff a silk blouse into the pocket of a raincoat on an adjacent rack in hopes of retrieving it the next day when it is due for its second markdown. All the stories are true. As a common community activity, hitting the Basement rivals following the Red Sox. It's another one of the reasons some people can't leave Boston.

William Filene established Filene's in 1881. His son Edward developed the Basement over a ten-year period about the turn of the century. New Yorkers buy it wholesale. We don't need to.

F ill. If it's flat, it's probably been added. Since 1804, Boston's original peninsula has increased threefold in acreage as the coves and the marshes were filled. Back Bay, Bay Village, parts of South Boston, and the South End are all filled land. Mass General, *The Boston Globe,* Faneuil Hall Marketplace, South Station, the airport, M.I.T., and all the buildings on Beacon Hill between Charles Street and the river are on fill. Filled land requires special construction techniques. The John Hancock Tower was anchored by piles driven into bedrock. Other building foundations near tidewater resemble cofferdams holding back the sea. Still other buildings float like boats, with double basements.

Older buildings within filled areas stand on wooden piles immersed in water, which prevents the piles from rotting. For a number of years officials at Trinity Church checked its 4,500 piles by rowing a small boat beneath the church. Due to disputed causes, the water table drops periodically in some filled areas, causing furors. The last furor on the flat part of Beacon Hill was complicated by threats from an employee in the city's inspectional services department. He claimed that the houses were ready to topple and threatened to condemn them. Many owners found their support piles were in trouble and fixed them for as much as several hundreds of thousands of dollars. But the city employee was later hauled into court for taking kickbacks from contractors. Skeptical inhabitants who had long ago grown used to the creative angles with which their walls met their floors wondered about some connection between the kickbacks and the new work homeowners were prodded into doing.

State legislation now effectively bars filling any wetlands in Massachusetts. Barring providential acts, Boston is the size and shape it's going to be.

Fire. When we mention hot cars, we're not just talking theft: the car's probably on fire. People grow tired of making payments on their cars, so they torch them. This subterfuge is better than the one they used to resort to. In the 1960s and 1970s, arsonists burned houses. The city was on the skids and lots of buildings were vacant. The biggest Massachusetts miracle is that a combination of a strong economy, rising property values, and effective arson investigations has made arson decline remarkably. You're no longer sure to wake up to a fire on your street every night.

Nevertheless, Massachusetts still spends a lot more on fire protection than the average state—$71 per person, compared to an average of $40 elsewhere, in one recent count. We also have more than double the national average of firefighters per person. We need them. It's harder to get to fires over our narrow twisting streets that are usually blocked by a couple of illegally parked cars. The population density makes for greater danger if a fire breaks out. The wood-frame buildings in the annexed areas of the city burn easily. Because of the haphazardly arranged fire escapes and safe exits, Boston firefighters are known for their skill and reliance on ladder work, as well as their courage in entering the burning building.

Fire is in our blood. The wood-framed buildings in the colonial city were regularly consumed. The British burned Charlestown after they decided they didn't like the way they were being treated at the Battle of Bunker Hill. The 1872 fire burned more buildings than the Chicago fire in the same decade. The Cocoanut Grove night club burned in 1942, killing 491 people and inspiring new fire laws requiring doors that open out and emergency lighting. Arthur Fiedler, long the conductor of the Pops, symbolized Boston's special relationship with fire when he rode around in fire engines decked out in full regalia.

Firsts. Here's what Boston had and what Bostonians did before other Americans got to it. The first black regiment in the north—during the Civil War. The first public school—1635. The first black-white integrated church—the First Baptist Free Church. The first botanical garden—the Arnold Arboretum. The first use of ether as an anesthetic—in the Bulfinch Building of the Massachusetts General Hospital. The first bicycle club—1879 at 87 Summer Street. The first campus established by a Japanese university—the Showa Women's Institute in Jamaica Plain in 1988. The first library to hire a woman for its professional staff— the Boston Athenaeum. The first intelligible voice transmission by telephone—from Alexander Graham Bell to Thomas A. Watson. The first boy's choir—at the Advent Church. The first use of the plastic bag to collect, store, and transfuse blood—by Dr. Carl Walter at the Peter Bent Brigham Hospital. The publishing of the first architectural periodical—*The American Architect and Builder.* The first apartment house—the Hotel Pelham. The first state to issue license plates. The first height limitation on buildings. The first state board of health. The first organized football team—a neighborhood group on Boston Common. The first auto insurance—this is the first place that needed it. The first railroad—between Quincy and Boston in 1826. The first portion of the Bible translated into an Indian language. The first grand opera sung in

Italian in the United States. The first surviving Anglican church in America—King's Chapel. The first Unitarian church in America—King's Chapel. The first airport chapel—Our Lady of the Airways in Terminal C. The first implantation of an artifical aortic valve—at Peter Bent Brigham Hospital. The first Audubon society. The first chocolate factory—Baker's Chocolate in Dorchester. The first arts and crafts society. The first medical school to admit women—Boston University. The first public beach. The first newspaper in the New World—*Public Occurances Both Forreign and Domesticke,* 1690. The home of the first American-born professional architect—Charles Bulfinch. The first city to establish free public baths. The first conservation land trusts. The first metropolitan park system. The first public transit line to serve a major airport. The first savings bank—the Provident Institution for Savings. The first pianoforte factory. The first statute against cruelty to animals. The first singing of "My Country 'Tis of Thee"—July 4, 1832, at the Park Street Church. The first book printed in British America—*The Bay Psalm Book,* in Cambridge by printer Stephen Daye in 1638. The first use of booing to indicate disapproval—at the opening of *The Playboy of the Western World,* by the Irish playwright John Millington Synge, attended by both Isabella Stewart Gardner and Rose Fitzgerald Kennedy, neither of whom booed. The first high-technology office park at a major United States international airport—the one-million-square-foot Massachusetts Technology Center on the old Bird Island Flats.

Fish Piers. The Chesapeake has its watermen, Long Island has its baymen. The people who fish out of Massachusetts Bay have no special name. They are called simply fishermen. For a major seacoast city, Boston has a small fishing fleet— an assortment of lobster boats and fishing boats that go out to George's Bank with a small crew to fish for a declining catch of cod, flounder, pollock, haddock, and whiting. New Bed-

51

ford, a small city in southeastern Massachusetts, is the port handling the largest dollar value in the nation because of its sea-scallop catch. The New Bedford port is grimy and industrial, not the quaint little fishing village that New England postcards like to tout. Gloucester is the town to see if you want a real fishing port with character. Boston Harbor, though it is a major fresh-fish distribution center, always had priorities other than fishing, notably shipping.

Fishing is seven times more dangerous than the average for all other industries. Regulation is spotty. Fishermen work long hours and stay out ten days at a time. But it's an exciting, independent life. The harbor fishing industry was born again after Congress passed the 1976 law declaring that waters within 200 miles of our shores were reserved for American boats. Fishermen bought new boats. Younger people confidently went into the industry. The catch is down, but prices are high and eating fish has become a healthful habit.

The fresh fish auction takes place every day between Anthony's and Jimmy's Restaurants on Northern Avenue between Fort Point Channel and South Boston at 6:30 A.M. The fish pier is a rehab, as are the condominiums that also hug the harbor. The housing interests and the harbor industrial uses are in a tug of war. How much of the harbor will be reserved for traditional harbor activities—fishing, lobstering, shipping, and boat repair—industries that must have water frontage? How much will be given over to office buildings, condominiums, and museums, which could go elsewhere?

G **arbage Collection.** This is one of the two city services—the other is fire protection— that works reliably. Sometimes we wish it didn't. You can tell when it's garbage-collection day. The streets are noisier than usual and they are lined with cars whose progress is blocked by the bulky trucks.

Frequent garbage collection is a blessing for people who lack alleys in which to store garbage containers. The problem is that garbage collection adds to the garbage on the streets. Imagine trying to keep a street clean on which dogs and unmentionable rodents are treated to thrice weekly opportunities to rip open plastic bags. Imagine the debris that collects where city workers are tossing garbage around every other day. The next day's garbage collection is another reason not to clean up.

G **arden, the.** As in Boston Garden, that cramped, low-tech, overgrown box with no air-conditioning at North Station serving both the Celtics and the Bruins. Definite plans threaten to redo it. But the one we have now is pure Boston. It has the same qualities as Fenway Park—center-city location, uncomfortable seats, and a paint job several years old. Without those, the Celtics might never win again. The Bruins would probably have to move. Just compare those two beloved Garden inhabitants to our football team, whatever its name is, which set up shop somewhere in a new stadium south of the city. Just getting out of the parking lot takes two hours. Bostonians don't really care about those games unless they have a bet riding on the point spread. But the Celtics and the Bruins, like the Red Sox, are our heart and soul. They're right here among us acting like real Bostonians.

General, the. Massachusetts General Hospital accepted its first patient in 1821. It now encompasses twenty-one acres on Cambridge Street in part of the old West End. It is one of the hospitals affiliated with Harvard Medical School, whose students call Mass. General the "massive genital." The General is only one of about 100 hospitals in the metropolitan area. Boston hospitals probably give no better care than hospitals anywhere. Some patients, in fact, swear the care is worse. The key to Boston medicine is not care, but cure.

If a disease can be cured, a Boston doctor may know how to do it better than doctors in other places. The reason is research. Brigham and Women's Hospital, a Harvard affiliate, receives more funding than any other independent hospital in the nation. When the research funds pulled in by Harvard and all its affiliated hospitals are totaled, it's more than twice as great as any other city gets. The Harvard figure doesn't count the significant funding that Tufts and Boston University and their hospitals receive. No wonder that the *New England Journal of Medicine,* the most prestigious medical periodical in the world, is located here. Research also goes on privately at the biotechnology companies around M.I.T. and the hospitals and on Route 128.

The heavy emphasis on research and the close affiliation with the teaching hospitals does strange things to doctors. It gives them good tools like artificial skin; a device that captures and reuses a patient's own blood during a heart operation; and an infusion pump for delivering chemotherapeutic agents to the liver. It also

54

makes them less rich. In some of the small and poorer cities of America, one can always recognize doctors. They are the ones in the Mercedes. Massachusetts doctors drive cars more like everyone else's, for their incomes are only 79 percent as great as the national average. They need the money, because they must pay back the $70,000 in debt that the average medical student accumulates. Some doctors complain that heavy regulation and insurance costs unfairly limit their incomes. Others point out that part of the problem for doctors is the massive competition—the ratio here of doctors to residents is 46 percent above the national average. Part of the problem is also the Boston physician's way of spending time—procedures, such as operations and administration of anesthesia, provide more income than teaching or searching for the cancer cure, unless, of course, one finds it. It's still hard to find surgeons who are suffering economically, but researchers are paid relatively low salaries by the hospitals. Some at middle age still work the emergency room on a beeper to make up the difference.

The hospitals' problems are similar to those in other Boston industries. They need more real estate. The General has outgrown its quarters and has moved major research arms to the Charlestown Navy Yard. The Longwood area, which includes Brigham and Women's Hospital, Children's Hospital, the Dana-Farber Cancer Institute, and the Harvard Medical School, among other institutions, takes up more than the equivalent of fifteen blocks. It qualifies as a small city in more ways than just size and population, which exceeds 20,000. The Longwood hospitals grew tired of Boston's regarding street signs as an unnecessary frill. They took matters into their own hands, installing bright blue street signs on every corner. It's now the only place in the city in which you know exactly where you are.

G **eneral Court, the.** The Massachusetts legislature, consisting of the House and the Senate, take its name from pre-Revolutionary predecessor. Out of pride or misinformation, many call this body The Great and General Court. It meets at the State House, the Bay Stater's name for the capitol building. Democrats outnumber Republicans in the General Court by almost four to one. The last Republican governor, who elsewhere might look suspiciously like a Democrat, was ousted in 1974. Massachusetts became attached to one-party politics in state elections because the Irish and the Yankees finally saw eye to eye.

In nineteenth century Boston, the Yankee Republican Party promoted government action, righting such wrongs as slavery and regulating commercial life for the condition that was determined to be the common good. The Democrats at the time were more hands-off. Because the Irish had learned back in the old country to distrust governments, they liked the Democratic Party's attitude. They also wanted to make sure they were on a different side from the Yankees, who were not exactly cordial to the new arrivals. Later Irish immigrants had little political choice. The old Irish ward bosses, in exchange for helping the immigrants get jobs, housing, food, and a good funeral, signed them up as Democrats as soon as they got off the boat.

The national parties gradually changed. The Republicans became more laissez-faire and the Democrats became the party of intervention. And so the old local alliances shifted. Yankees still believed in government action to right wrongs and regulate commercial life. They found themselves unwelcome in the changing Republican party. They were more and more likely to vote Democratic. The Irish discovered that as they took over local government, it worked well for them and they trusted it more; they remained Democrats. Today's Republicans seeking state office have made it easy for the Democrats to stay on top. They have fielded candidates with colorful lives—fake college degrees, among dates with colorful lives—fake college degrees, among other credentials, and flirtations with the ultraconservative John Birch Society, which began in Belmont, Massachusetts. In a recent election, one Republican gubernatorial candidate was reported to be prowling the halls in a downtown office building without clothes. Another claimed he'd seen action in Vietnam, only to admit later he'd seen the action only on television. One State House wag thereupon called the Republicans the party of the naked and the dead. With the Republicans providing the entertainment the Democrats used to dish out, it may take another social revolution to even things up.

Getting on the State. Want a job? Your brother-in-law will put in a word for you. "Getting on the state" is the time-honored Boston welfare system for the middle class. It used to be said that whole sections of the city were employed by government. But that was when government jobs paid well compared to private industry. The practice originated out of necessity. Throughout Boston in the early years of immigration, signs too often proclaimed "No Irish Need Apply." The Irish found jobs in government instead. In some neighborhoods the number of public servants is still high: 20 percent of the working men and women in West Roxbury and South Boston are employed by the government, including the mayor of the city and the state senate president.

It's still a good idea in Boston to "get on the state," and for the same reasons as always. State government in recent years has been seen as one employer that would provide reliable, equal opportunity. City government also has a growing reputation for color and ethnic blindness. Recently the percentage of government employees in neighborhoods settled predominantly by newer black and Hispanic immigrants has been rising almost as high as in the traditional "getting on the state" neighborhoods.

Getting There. All natives carry detailed maps of the metropolitan area in their cars, because they can't get there any better than any one else. One problem is that almost all downtown Boston streets are one-way, requiring careful plotting and intricate backtracking to reach one's intended destination. Another puzzler is that streets in different parts of the city carry the same name. Seven streets are named Mt. Vernon, and so you'd better know whether you want the one in Charlestown or the one in West Roxbury, not to mention those in South Boston, Beacon Hill, Dorchester, or Columbia Point, before you head out.

Another problem is traffic jams that tie up the whole city. These are explainable when you understand Boston habits: An executive on her way to the airport abandoned her car in the Callahan Tunnel when it ran out of gas. She had no time to take care of it because she had a meeting in New York at nine o'clock. Any Boston driver would have done the same. Duration of traffic jam: two hours.

Boston and Massachusetts have the greatest number of traffic accidents in the United States. The most entertaining ones involve the heavy rigs trying to make up for lost time that overturn on the Southeast Expressway. These trucks sometimes require removal by helicopter. Duration of jam: up to six hours.

Trucks on Storrow Drive weekly get lodged under the bridges. The drivers don't believe the signs that brush the tops of their cabs proclaiming LOW CLEARANCE—10 FEET. Why should they? Most other Boston traffic signs, if you can find them, are wrong. At the road leading from Alewife Station onto Route 2, the top sign says, NO TURNS. The second sign down says,

LEFT TURN ONLY. Both are wrong. A Storrow Drive sign points you to DOWNTOWN, but in fact, it spills you into Back Bay.

Street names may change without warning every few blocks. But you'll never know, because thoroughfares are not marked, on the principle that if you're on it, you must know what it is. The truth you must face in Boston about getting there is that you can't, at least not from here.

G lass. Boston has had bad luck with glass. A shipment with no quality control came over from England early in the nineteenth century and gradually turned purple. After a hundred years or so, the mistake made purple glass THE kind to have. Only four Beacon Hill houses survive with the original panes, but because purple panes automatically make any room more desirable, you'll find copies here and there. When quality control was a problem for the John Hancock Insurance Company it did what any twentieth-century red-blooded American company would do—it sued. And then it kept the cause of the problem and the results of the suit quiet. Therefore we know only part of the story. The new John Hancock Insurance Company building, designed by I. M. Pei & Partners, was under construction in January 1973 when many of its 10,344 mirrored glass panes began cracking and falling to the sidewalk. Hancock hired spotters with field glasses who all day scanned the façade for cracks so that workmen could remove the offending pane before it crashed below. Instead of glass, the tower soon was sheathed in plywood. Pedestrians avoided the area. Analysis began. A slew of engineers and experts, including one flown over from Switzerland and one brought in from Western Ontario, studied the difficulty. They soon found a problem more threatening than the glass—namely, that the building itself might fall. Workers installed additional steel to "stiffen the spine." The original plate glass was replaced. Panes still crack. The only hope for John Hancock now is to go the purple glass route. If it can hold out until the cracking becomes historic, cracked glass could become THE kind to have.

Grazing. It is not true that Boston citizens are still allowed to graze their cows on the Common. The only one who can do that nowadays is the American Dairy Association, which shows up each June. We wouldn't want to move our cows to the Common even if we had any. Boston citizens consider it cruelty to animals to subject them to a ride on Boston streets.

Green. The Celtics, the Monster, the real grass at Fenway Park, St. Patrick's Day, the Emerald Necklace, the copper roofs and trim. Boston's unofficial color is green. If you decide to run for office in this city, make your announcement first so that you can have first dibs on green for your bumper stickers and yard signs.

H **arbor, the.** You think traffic on the Southeast Expressway is bad. Just wait till you get on a boat in Boston Harbor. Sailboats to the left of you, cruise ships to the right of you. And what seem like six hundred water taxis circling. But the breeze is in your face and a coffee cup and a newspaper are in your hand. No one has found a better way to relax, commute, or get to the airport in Boston than via the harbor.

For many years, Bostonians saw the harbor as a blight, not an asset. It took up too much room, so early Bostonians filled it in. The harbor was a commercial success until the mid-nineteenth century, when shipping began to move to New York. The harbor began a hundred-year decline. World War II brought some maritime activity back, but by the late 1960s, the shipbuilding industry was gone, commercial shipping facilities were hopelessly dated, cruise ships had deleted Boston from their schedules, and government officials were too busy building the airport to care. Rotting warehouses and chain-link fences crowded the shore, blocking access to the sea. Facilities for fishermen and lobstermen were falling down. The only way anyone could tell that Boston was a coastal town was when the sea breeze blew all the way into the neighborhoods, coughing up a Bostonian's favorite aroma of seaweed, dying fish, and salt.

Circumstances happily changed. When new high-rises went up, office workers saw the view and said, "Well, look what we have here." Prosperity came. The city and real-estate developers hit on the harbor as a good place for offices and housing to expand. Lobster facilities were planned, the Fish Pier was renovated, and up-to-date containerized shipping facilities and a cruise-ship terminal were built. Commuter boats were brought in. The old wharves were rebuilt and opened to the public. The state government finally persuaded enough of the harbor's communities to cooperate so that real clean-up could begin. Now everyone wants to be on the harbor. Boston has become a seacoast city once again.

Hardiness. It is expected that a New Englander will prevail over circumstances and the elements. Here are a few of the beliefs we hold dear: Winter is invigorating. The cold North Atlantic waters make the swimming healthier and the fish taste better. The five-story climb from the kitchen to the baby's bedroom is aerobic. Walking is healthier than driving. Looking for parking builds character. Outwitting car thieves sharpens the senses. We never liked spring anyway. Having to respond to rudeness, surliness, and hostility sharpens your reaction time. Sitting in traffic is educational. Dealing with City Hall and the Registry of Motor Vehicles keeps you on your toes. New England cooking keeps you in touch with the basics. New Englanders are tough and have character, if not God, on their side. Don't tangle with them.

Heels. Shoe-repair shops thrive in Boston as nowhere else. This industry owes its success to bricks and municipal neglect. City contractors save money and time by laying sidewalk bricks too far apart. Then the city refuses to maintain them; it has more important things to do like waiting for potholes to appear in the streets. Bricks may be beautiful to Bostonians, but they ruin shoes. Any woman wearing high heels will catch her heel, maybe sprain her ankle, but certainly mangle the leather beyond repair. One wearing and that's it for a pair of shoes. Men don't get off easily, either. The uneven sidewalks tear into soles so that within a few weeks, low-heeled shoes need an overhaul. The situation is so desperate, it's a wonder no one has yet established the perfect Boston store—a combination while-you-wait shoe-repair shop and bookstore—treating two Boston necessities simultaneously.

Historic Districts. Also known as "Hysteric Districts" because of the regrettable reaction when, after one spends $1.6 million for a small brick abode, one finds one cannot, without permission, paint one's own front door. In a historic district, the visible exteriors of buildings are protected. All proposed changes must be reviewed by the local architectural commission to determine if the change is in keeping with the neighborhood's historic quality. Boston has eight historic districts, protecting about 7,500 buildings or a little more than 6 percent of the number in the city. Beacon Hill, designated in the 1950s, was the first historic district north of the Mason-Dixon line.

Cambridge has two historic districts and two neighborhood conservation districts with lesser protections. The home of two major schools of architecture, Cambridge takes historic design seriously. The Cambridge Historic Commission has a record of every building in the city, complete with photograph, construction dates, and sometimes other historical information. For a small fee, the commission consults with homeowners on changes and works out appropriate paint schemes.

When an owner in either city doesn't follow the rules, the courts can be harsh. One downtown condominium developer flouted the rules and was ordered to remove the illegally constructed top floor.

Once you've lived in a historic district, you feel naked without the protection. After all, if you do spend a huge sum on a piece of property, it's nice to know someone else is out there helping to keep the value up. History is worth money in Boston.

Hub. Boston would never lay claim to being the "clam capital of the world." That would be too unsophisticated. It would never call itself the "friendliest town in America." That would be an outright lie. Instead, Boston modestly claims it's the "Hub of the Universe." Never mind that Boston is a middling-sized city up in the far corner of a big country. The facts have never stopped its inhabitants from regarding all other locations as out of the way.

Oliver Wendell Holmes (the father, doctor, and author, not the son who was the justice) was the first to offer this description when he declared in 1858 in *The Autocrat of the Breakfast Table* that "Boston Statehouse is the hub of the solar system." Later writers boiled Holmes's description down to its essence and it has been in use ever since.

It should be. Boston's intellectual life is unsurpassed. Its cultural offerings are unparalleled. It succeeds in aesthetic city planning. Its medical establishment is the finest. Its financial ingenuity knows no bounds. Its business acumen is the most up-to-date. Its politics are the most colorful. If the city does not shine at an endeavor, it's because the endeavor is tasteless, anti-intellectual, valueless, or illegal. It is, Bostonians believe, the most civilized city in the New World. The English philosopher Alfred North Whitehead likened Boston to the Paris of the Middle Ages. Bostonians believe that his was faint praise.

I **ngenuity.** The Massachusetts coastline was not the most economically promising. Its terrain was too rocky for successful farming and offered few raw materials. Its growing season was shortened by ice-bound winters. The rivers were too shallow for navigation. What did the old Yankees do? Quarried the granite, dammed the rivers for power, shipped other countries' goods, and sold the ice to tropical lands. They even made ice cream to show equatorial peoples why they needed the ice. So reports Samuel Eliot Morison, New England's own private historian with national stature.

Later Yankees invented the telephone, the safety razor, Fig Newtons, a silk purse made from a sow's ear, instant photography, Christian Science, kidney transplants, toll-house cookies, the wooden golf tee, a machine that reads and another that writes, ether, a home test for strep throat, a lead balloon, a plastic pencil, and a recording device that fends off squirrels at the Harvard Business School.

I **rish.** The Irish, at 21 percent of the population, outnumber other nationalities in Boston. They are famed for politics and wit. The most notorious display of these Irish talents is at the St. Patrick's Day breakfast held annually since 1948. The menu: corned beef, cabbage, green beer, and local public figures. The place is jammed and so the famous and

65

nearly-famous must enter and exit by fire escape. Billy Bulger, the senate president, is the host and master of ceremonies. He makes the same jokes from year to year because everyone prefers it that way. And everyone is fair game.

The senate president gives it to the Yankees for their parochialism:

One time when I was in Los Angeles, I called Mr. Saltonstall, and his Aunt Abigail answered. "Why, William, where are you?" asks Aunt Abigail. Mindful that Aunt Abigail recognizes only the thirteen original colonies, I say, "I'm 'way out in Los Angeles." "How is it out there?" she asks. "It's warm," I say. "Of course it's warm, William," says Aunt Abigail. "You're 3,000 miles from the ocean."

He rags the Irish, too:

A guy in Ireland pulls into a petrol station. "Fill up my car with some petrol," he says. "We don't have any," says the attendant. "All right, then, I'd like some oil." "We don't have any of that, either." "No petrol? No oil? What kind of a petrol station is this anyway?" asks the guy. "We're not a petrol station. We're a front for the IRA," says the attendant. "All right, then blow up my tires."

The senate president on the business world:

They call it the triangular trade route. You go from the Harvard Business School to Wall Street to the witness protection program.

He impugns the intelligence of a former Democratic governor who became a Republican:

A few years ago, I went in to see the governor. I wanted to put in twelve gondolas down in the Public Garden and the Common to take tourists around. The governor was on this big kick for austerity. I said, "Governor, I'd like twelve gondolas." Then I explained my plan. The governor said, "No, no. Get two gondolas, one male and one female. Then let mother nature take her course."

Then the senate president talks about sin, everyone's favorite topic:

In County Mayo, a fellow is going up a holy mountain on his knees as an act of penance, along with a lot of other people. A lady is right ahead of him. She gets her heel caught in the hem of her dress and she can't get it free. She turns to the fellow and says, "Sir, would you be kind enough to lift me dress?" The fellow says, "I'll do nothing of the sort. It's for doing that that I'm doing this."

Irritability. Bostonians have been accused of possessing a hostile attitude toward the human race. It's untrue. The only people we don't like are tourists, patrons of public concerts, our neighbors, ballgame fans unless we're going, other drivers, the people who string the Christmas lights badly on the trees on the Common, customers, all politicians, and each other. We're not the kind of people from whom you can easily borrow a cup of sugar. We bristle when people compare us to those legendary irritants, New Yorkers and the French. We're not like them—we're ruder.

Like most other Boston characteristics, it's a tradition. Henry Adams called it "Bostonitis," and attributed it to "knowing too much of one's neighbors and thinking too much of oneself." He might have been right then, but he's wrong now. Our present problem is that we have a lot to contend with. The street is our garage. How would you like it if 33,000 Red Sox fans wanted to park in your garage? The Esplanade is our back yard. What would you think if 250,000 people wanted to celebrate the Fourth around your picnic table? Try driving here. If you let another car ahead of you in line, everyone else will try to crowd in too, which just shows you where generosity gets you. Unlike New York we're not big enough or beleaguered enough to feel that since it's so bad, why not enjoy it? We would never take the attitude we're all in it together, because for more than a century we have taken pride in our fragmentation. Pass the time of day with people on the street we don't know? Not a chance.

Italians. The last immigrants to settle in the North End, successive catchbasin for the Puritans, the Irish, then the Jews. This neighborhood is one of Boston's most intensely ethnic, the only place for many years where cooks could find handfuls of fresh basil or a string of garlic. People on the street still speak Italian. The neighborhood still celebrates a plethora of feasts and festivals unique in the city. The North End is cut off from the rest of Boston by the Harbor and the Central Artery. The Artery may have destroyed a swath of downtown Boston but for many years it saved the North End for Italians. When other groups encroached, they came from the direction of the Waterfront, where a number of Boston's professionals moved during the early 1970s.

It wasn't only gentrification that challenged homogeneity in the North End. Italians were no different from any other group that ever landed in Boston Harbor. As they became successful and more American, they moved up and out. While the Irish trickled over to Charlestown or the southern tier of suburbs, the Italians went to East Boston and the northern suburbs. They formed produce and grocery supply companies. They went into the building trades and became contractors. They also went into politics. The North End population grew older. Almost all the schools closed.

We face once more Boston's essential dilemma: How can we preserve the best of our neighborhoods without destroying them? They are culturally and historically rich, supportive in time of need, close in spirit. But almost all belong to a narrowly defined group of people, whose interests are more than likely to clash with those of the next neighborhood. More than other cities in North America, Boston continues to be fragmented. We struggle toward learning how to find for ourselves an American, not an ethnic, definition.

Japan. The relationship Boston has had with Japan is unique among American cities. It started in the late-nineteenth century, after Japan opened its doors to the West. Some historians believe that an immersion in Japanese culture provided an escape for Boston Brahmins, who saw their own influence waning as other groups gained power in the city.

Several Bostonians went to live in Japan for a number of years, collecting artwork and household objects and experimenting with Buddhism. The Bostonians admired Japan's excellence in the arts, its industrial efficiency, and its respect for ancestors. They saw Japanese society as similar to their own. The interest in Japan went beyond the Brahmins and the nineteenth century. The twentieth-century Mayor Curley welcomed a Japanese delegation to Boston, calling them the "Yankees of the East." It is assumed that he meant the remark as a compliment.

Between the World Wars, when hostility and suspicion toward the Japanese were growing in other parts of the country, Bostonians continued to promote Japan and safeguard its culture. During the war, when a number of dolls the Japanese had presented to museums throughout the United States were destroyed, the Boston Children's Museum resisted those influences and saved its doll, which is still on display. The Japanese–New England link continues unabated. Because of the nineteenth-century Bostonians' collections, the Museum of Fine Arts has the most distinguished collection of Japanese artifacts outside of Japan. The Peabody Museum in Salem also has extensive Japanese holdings. Kyoto, an important university center, is Boston's sister city. Japan gave Boston the cherry trees along the Charles in 1984; in a few years, they ought to rival Washington D. C.'s show of color. The Children's Museum has had an important Japanese exhibit for many years. In 1979, a Kyoto delegation was disappointed that the museum had only a tea room. So the delegation sent Boston a whole house, 150 years old, which the city turned over to the museum. It has a television and a modern kitchen, as well as traditional objects, showing visitors how a Japanese family would live in it today.

Jimmies. The grandaddy of ice-cream toppings, claimed by Brigham's, a Boston-area ice-cream and restaurant company in business since 1914. Company records don't reveal why these miniature chocolate sausages were named "jimmies." But with or without an explanation for their name, jimmies matter to Bostonians because we consume more ice cream per person than any other city in the world. So also do New Englanders in general—twenty-three quarts per person per year compared to fifteen quarts per person in the rest of America. This figure seems high until you look at how much alcohol we take in—about forty-four gallons per adult, also a record-breaker.

Besides jimmies, Bostonians have a few other peculiarities in their ice-cream habits. Though most of the rest of the country calls an ice cream shake a milkshake, we call it a "frappe," a French word referring to a semifrozen mixture. If you ask for a milkshake in a traditional New England ice-cream store, you will get just that—milk and syrup shaken together.

Bailey's, another local nineteenth-century ice-cream and candy emporium still in existence, claims to have invented the hot-fudge sundae. Howard Johnson's, now just a lick of its former self, made offering a myriad of flavors the ice-cream vendor's standard. Its first restaurant was just south of Boston. Boston is now a center for boutique ice cream. Stores selling ice cream are almost as plentiful as those selling books.

Julia. The British didn't do it. The Irish were no help. The French never got here in the critical mass we needed. Even the Italians and the Chinese were unable to influence the situation. To finally bring good food to Boston, it took a well-traveled Californian with a sympathetic accent, interest in food scholarship, and careless disregard for sartorial splendor. Julia Child was someone who spoke the Boston language.

B.J. (Before Julia), the best we did was in 1794 when chef Jean Baptiste Gilbert Payplat escaped from the Paris mobs, renamed himself Julien, and set up the Restorator. For thirty years this restaurant allowed Bostonians to reach French gastronomic heights. Boston's Anglophilia (see *Anglophilia*), however, eventually prevailed, with Bostonians taking on British taste buds along with more laudable characteristics. Puritan suspicion of anything potentially pleasurable also affected Bostonians' attitude toward eating. While a few other American cities were cultivating a cuisine, Boston brushed off food as a necessity, not an art form. (Look into an old copy of the Boston Cooking School's *Fannie Farmer Cookbook,* which had a claim to fame: standardized measurement. It is, well, basic.) As long as no one tried to cook it, the food was okay. Not by accident, the oldest city restaurant is the Union Oyster House, established in 1826, with its own specialty, oysters and clams served raw.

Boston was ready for Julia when she arrived. The city had access to marvelous ingredients, especially the fish and shellfish from cold waters, the condition that gourmets believe is best for taste. It had an assortment of immigrants from all nations who, once the idea took hold, could offer their finest talents. And it had a growing population from the rest of country who came and asked, "Why don't you have more good restaurants here?" Now we do, including some who do lobster like it's never been done and one named after the original Boston French chef, Julien.

Julia—we all call her that, whether we know her or not—lives for part of the year in a professor-infested Cambridge enclave and got her television start on public channel WGBH, the only local station any cultivated Bostonian admits to watching. She has published a number of cookbooks. She herself believes that out of necessity, Boston's food efforts went into preserving, rather than cooking food, because of the short growing season. What Julia did for Boston, she also did for the rest of America. Bon appétit.

K **arma.** Why would any civilized person put up with Boston's traffic, trash, haphazard services, complaining, and complete anarchy? Not every civilized person can. It's only those who have a good karma who survive the cosmic aggravations in this city. Good karmas bring justice. They bring peace. Karmas are a fitting antidote to chaos in a city once richly populated by Brahmins.

A good parking karma gets you a place in a city where at any one time 1,130 people are driving around looking for one. A good justice karma is operating when you arrive home to find a burglar on the third floor stealing the jewelry left to you by your grandmother. You call the police, but, as a precaution, you shout to the city workers fixing three lamps in front of your building to catch the thief if he tries to get down the stairs. He does, and they do, and by the time the police arrive, the burglar is lying on the ground with three people sitting on him. You know your karma is working because it was you who staged a sit-in and threatened to sue unless those lights were repaired.

Your karma is working when you're in your city garden at dusk. The subway train is grinding by, the ambulances scream into the nearby hospital, the neighbor's dog is barking, and the jets from Logan have changed their path so that they're right over your house. You think your mother was right when she begged you to move to Wellesley. You look up. Above you glides the silent Goodyear blimp, lit up in jewel lights for the evening.

Without your karma, life would be too hard. But if your karma is in shape, you can make it in downtown Boston.

Kennedys. Kennedys or their forebears have been running for public office in Massachusetts (and, more recently, Rhode Island) since late in the nineteenth century, and they show no signs of letting up on the family business. Locally, they are impossible to beat, although a few brave souls try. At home, they made being Irish and Catholic not only socially acceptable, but esteemed. Elsewhere, they replaced the image Americans have of Boston as tight-lipped Brahmin territory that looks back, with a new view of vigor and volubility in the self-made who look forward. (Never mind that the presidential generation of Kennedys and their offspring are hardly self-made; they are still vigorous.)

The Kennedy story is in some ways typical for an Irish family in Boston. Their ancestors came here in the mid-nineteenth century fleeing starvation in Ireland. They settled in the North End and East Boston and prospered in politics and business. Rose Kennedy's father, Honey Fitz, was mayor of Boston; Patrick Kennedy, the president's grandfather, owned several taverns and founded a bank. The president's father, Joseph Patrick Kennedy, was the first in his family to go to Harvard, graduating in 1912. Other young Irish men by then were going there, too. Joseph P. Kennedy made a fortune and made it possible for his descendants to practice politics.

In their national prominence, and apparently their longevity, the Kennedy family most resembles the Adamses. The Adams influence on national affairs has extended over two centuries. Two Adamses signed the Declaration of Independence. Two were presidents of the United States. Three were ambassadors to England. One was a renowned author. A twentieth-century Adams was president of the Raytheon Corporation.

Kettle Holes. Boston's terrain is a product left by four glaciers that advanced and retreated, the last one leaving the area about 12,000 years ago. Jamaica Pond in Jamaica Plain is a kettle hole, scooped out by the ice sheet. The harbor islands and the other hills around Boston are drumlins formed by the melting glacier dropping debris around sticky clay deposits. The glacier defined general outlines for Cape Cod, Nantucket, and Martha's Vineyard. It also left the boulders and rocks that have been used to make the endless rows of stone walls all over New England. The early farmers had to remove the stones from the fields before they could till the soil.

Underlying the carved landscape in some places is Roxbury pudding stone, a conglomerate or pressed sedimentary mixture that adorns the Church of the Holy Bean Blowers or the First Baptist Church on Commonwealth Avenue at Clarendon Street and other buildings. We also have granite, especially in Quincy, which provided the material for King's Chapel, the Bunker Hill Monument, and Quincy Market. Although it suffered from the same glacial scraping as other parts of the United States and Canada, Boston is geologically not a part of North America. It is believed to be part of the Avalon microcontinent, a sliver of land that formed after the North American and European continents separated about 650 million years ago. The original parcel included parts of the British Isles, Newfoundland, Nova Scotia, New Brunswick, and the Carolinas. The Boston Basin was severed from the other locations and eventually became attached to North America.

The water in New England is soft because we have no vast underlying limestone deposits to harden it. That's good for keeping bathtubs clean and conserving on soap. It's also good for dogwoods and rhododendrons, which like acid soil. It's bad for lawns, foxgloves, and most vegetables, which thrive in limey soil. New England gardeners buy a lot of lime to give plants a boost.

Earthquakes shake New England about twenty-five to thirty times a year. The area around Boston is one of most active in the East for small earthquakes. Because of the region's geology, the earthquakes are felt over a wider area than quakes in other parts of North America. The Massachusetts building code since 1975 has required some earthquake protection. Boston is especially vulnerable because of the large number of buildings on filled land, which can increase groundshaking intensity.

Kiosks. Of the two kiosks Bostonians can't do without one satisfies our wide interests. The antique newsstand in the middle of Harvard Square sells magazines and newspapers from all over the United States and the world. The other satisfies our parsimony. This one is ArtsBoston at the edge of Quincy Market, which sells discounted tickets on the day of the performance. In a city known for its music, one kiosk stands too silent. On the Common is a deserted bandstand in ill repair. On a perfect Common, performers would crowd it every night.

L **anterns.** A vicious rumor is afloat that the signal lanterns warning Paul Revere about the British route were hung in the "Old North" of 1775, which later succumbed to the occupying British soldiers who tore it up for firewood. Our Old North was then New North or Christ Church.

Forget the rumors. The present Old North has a belfry arch well suited to lanterns and we prefer to imagine them winking there. For those who like lanterns, we have provided many charming ones along our streets. Hard to shut off and turn on without expensive equipment or daily tending, the gaslights in the downtown neighborhoods burn twenty-four hours a day.

L **atin.** Boston Latin, the first public school in the country, came into being one year before Harvard. If only it had fared as well as the younger institution. The early school taught Latin in order to prepare young men for Harvard. In its heyday Boston Latin educated illustrious men—John Hancock, Samuel Adams, Benjamin Franklin, Ralph Waldo Emerson, Henry Ward Beecher, and Honey Fitz, John Kennedy's grandfather. But in recent years, many Boston parents have lost confidence in the public schools. Nearly one-third of Boston's school-age children attend private or parochial schools.

Boston parents have had good reason to be suspicious of the Boston school system. The first problem is the

Boston School Committee—probably the least-respected body of public servants in the Commonwealth—which runs the Boston Public Schools. In luckier Massachusetts communities, the School Committee might have some members truly interested in education. But in Boston, over the years, the number of School-Committee members with educational interests can be counted on one hand. Most candidates for the School Committee see it as the entry point into Massachusetts politics. Because school-committee members have too often been indicted or found wanting in gray matter before they've had a chance to take their next step, most who run for the office automatically gets classified as dimwitted or half-crooked, just by seeking the job.

The next problem is the school system's recent history. Some years ago, the Boston School Committee and the school administration refused to deal with integration and maintained an obviously unequal system between blacks and whites. The courts ordered busing and took over the schools for many years. Boston survived integration and schools are no longer unequal. Bus problems, either with drivers striking or buses running late, have become one of the weakest parts of the system. Another problem is the schools' reputation. Several national magazines have called Boston's public school system the worst in the nation.

But no matter what grade the great schoolmaster in the sky gives Boston, one thing is sure. The Boston school system provides special education for 20 percent of its students under one of the most stringent special-education laws in the nation. The suspicion is that it doesn't do so badly in this regard. Maybe there's life in the old system yet.

Lobsters. Lobster is finger food. Here's how to eat one: Take one cooked lobster. A cooked lobster will be bright reddish orange, not dark reddish green. It will also be dead, whereas an uncooked lobster ought to be squirming until it is plunged alive into boiling seawater. Forget putting it out of its misery beforehand. New Englanders believe lobsters don't feel a thing. Have on hand a nutcracker, a nut pick, or a pickle fork, and plenty of napkins. Some restaurants provide bibs, which are not to be scorned.

With the nutcracker, crack the two parts of one of the lobster's front claws or pincers. Lift out the meat or pick it out with the nut pick. Dip the meat into lemon-butter sauce or clam broth and eat it. Do the same with the other claw. Dismember the joints leading to the claws and crack them too. Dig out the meat and eat.

Now take up the lobster in both hands and bend it back to separate the abdomen from the thorax or chest cavity. The lobster will disgorge juice and a greenish substance. Save the green. It's the tomalley or liver, which some people consider a great delicacy. Others, especially non-natives, can't abide it. If it's a female, the coral will also be present. This is the material from which the eggs will be made and is composed of small, red, angular pellets, somewhat waxy. Eat them.

Put the thorax aside for now. Take up the abdomen. Remove the fringed fans at the end of the tail and inspect them for meat. Pick it out with your nut pick if you find any. With the fans removed, you can push the abdomen meat—known colloquially as the tail—out of the shell with your fingers. You will have a nice hunk to chew on or, if you're fastidious, to cut up with a knife and fork and eat in bites. Continue dipping all pieces of meat into your broth or butter. Turn back to the thorax. On each side are four thin legs. Pull them from the lobster's body. New Englanders give these thin legs to small children who chew and suck on them. If no small children are about, pick out the meat yourself.

You are now left with the thorax, which has little meat. Most people quit here because after all that butter and lobster, they are stuffed. A few aficionados, however, will gather up everyone's leavings and sit for hours picking out all the meat the others left behind, after which they will make the next day's lobster stew.

Love Story. Boston looks better in the movies than it does in real life. Its colors are rich. The background is dense. The camera crew picks up the trash before they film the scene.

The Commonwealth is the fourth most common movie location after New York, California, and Florida. More than 125 films or television series have been made in Massachusetts since 1977, when the state film office began counting. *The Thomas Crown Affair* took place on Mount Vernon Street on Beacon Hill. "Spenser for Hire" was filmed all over Boston. *Jaws* took place on Martha's Vineyard. *International Velvet* (1978), *Home Before Dark* (1958), *Moby Dick* (1956), and *A Summer Place* (1959) were filmed here too. Probably the sappiest movie ever made here was *Love Story* (1970), filmed mostly in Cambridge.

When the film crews come to town, they move parked cars, stop traffic, and wet down the bricks to make them shinier. Being irritable, we complain about the disruption to our lives. But movie-making brings in $184 million annually to our economy. The money means never having to say we're sorry.

Ma. On most television sitcoms, American children call their female parent "Mom." Television writers spend too much time in Southern California. Massachusetts children and, in fact, most New England children, call their mothers "Ma." Unless they have grown to adulthood as upper-class Yankees, that is. Then, from Kennebunkport to Hyannisport, fifty-year-old men and women can be overheard referring to the seventy-five-year-old matriarch as "Mummy." It's one of the quaint customs. Get used to it.

Manhattanization. After traffic and parking, the most common subject of discussion in Boston. Everybody here is an amateur critic of architecture. (The Boston Society of Architects, the local American Institute of Architects affiliate, has almost as many nonarchitect members as it does professional architects.) The thing they criticize most is tall buildings.

The term "skyscraper" ought to be dear to Bostonians' hearts because, according to architectural historian Douglass Shand Tucci, it was first a nautical expression referring to the topmost sail on sailing ships, the nineteenth-century Boston trademark. Chicago's skyscraper pioneer, Louis Sullivan, was born here but left, claiming he didn't like the city's architecture.

The feeling was mutual. Boston's inhabitants resisted skyscrapers from at least 1904, when they clamped on a zoning restriction limiting the height of buildings in the business district to 125 feet and in residential sections to 80 feet. The law was modified in 1928 to allow for taller buildings if they were stepped back. Later, at the city's economic nadir, height restrictions were relaxed—some would say abandoned—in an attempt to pump vitality into a cause that appeared to be dying.

High-rise is still a cause for complaint. Some antagonists still focus on height. Others care more about the "stand-alone" quality of modern high-rises, which call attention to themselves at the expense of their surroundings. The two high-rises Bostonians seem to like best, the Hancock Tower in the Back Bay and the Federal Reserve Bank near South Station, have beautiful qualities, but their sidewalk perimeters are boring to the pedestrian, the most unforgivable mistake an architect in Boston can make. They're also too far back from the street.

Give us a door right at the sidewalk and we are happy. Give us a detail to look at as we pass by and we praise the architect. Give us crowded, close, tight buildings whose façades form a unified mass and we're right at home. In other words, give us buildings for walkers, not drivers.

If bland big buildings have a saving grace, it is their ability to make the old subtleties shine. Walk up State Street toward Congress. The walls of the high-rises are dark, bare, and cold. But in the center, lovely and unexpected as a lady's-slipper orchid in a forest, is the diminutive Old State House. It's the reason architecture was invented in the first place.

Maples. Sugar maples yield syrup in the spring and scarlet and gold leaves in the fall. They are one of dozens of varieties of trees that give Boston area parks and roadsides an impenetrable look. The best-loved may be the sycamores in Cambridge along the Charles near Harvard's Kennedy School. We also like the beeches in Brookline, the red oaks along the Arborway, and the sassafras trees behind the Longwood "T" stop on the Green Line. Hemlock Hill is in Jamaica Plain in the Arnold Arboretum, a botanical garden owned by Boston and run by Harvard. This stand of trees has not been cut and is probably the descendant of the original forest.

Bostonians love trees and the city is full of them at the moment. It hasn't always been that way. When the Puritans arrived, the land that would become the Common was a scruffy area with few trees. The Public Garden, now an arboreal showcase, was a tidal marsh. The colonists planted trees at the same time as they built their houses. In 1646, in a show of mutual endeavor probably not equaled since, every inhabitant of Boston helped plant dozens of elms along Boston Neck to retard erosion by the tides. Boston Neck was approximately where Washington Street and Essex Street are now. One of those elms later became known as the Liberty Tree. To protest against the Stamp Act in 1765, the Sons of Liberty hung in that elm effigies of the stamp collector, Andrew Oliver, and Lord Butte, the man believed to have been responsible for the Stamp Act. Towns all over America planted Liberty Trees to express sympathy with Boston. But the original Liberty Tree was cut down, as were almost all Boston's trees, by British soldiers desperate for firewood during the winter before they left Boston for good in March 1776. (The British were persuaded to leave when they noticed General Washington's fifty-nine cannon trained on their ships from Dorchester Heights, right over the harbor. General Washington had acquired these cannon from a young Boston bookseller, Henry Knox, who with a few men and some oxen, had dragged them hundreds of miles over the snow from Fort Ticonderoga to Boston in only two months. It was typical then, as it would be now in Boston, for this astonishing feat to have been brought about by a bookseller. Knox had learned about military matters by reading about them.)

After the war, while the rest of New England continued cutting down the forests, first for farming and then for lumber, Bostonians planted trees again, favoring chestnuts and elms. Nineteenth-century Bostonians were impressed with the size of trees. Oliver Wendell Holmes kept detailed records of the girth of elms he found. But the elms didn't last and neither did the chestnuts. Except for a few heavily inoculated elms, mostly in the Public Garden, they both succumbed to blights in the first part of the twentieth century, and the Boston landscape was severely damaged once again.

In the late 1960s and early 1970s, the Parks Department began vigorously planting pears, maples, lindens, pin oaks, gingkos, and honey locusts on the sidewalks, down the Commonwealth Avenue Mall, and in the parks. The wild Ailanthus, or tree of heaven, survived splendidly, if odoriferously, on its own.

The trees in the Public Garden and the Common are probably the oldest in the city, although no one knows for sure. Everyone who regularly strolls through the Public Garden has a few favorites. Look for two dawn redwoods—one on the Boylston Street side of George Washington's statue and the other between Beacon Street and the pond. Dawn redwoods, distinctive with their reddish braided trunks and feathery deciduous leaves, were thought to be extinct until 1947, when the Arnold Arboretum got word that a few trees had been found in China. The Arboretum sent a collector to gather seeds, from which grew these two trees, as well as hundreds of others now distributed across the United States.

Maps. If you're new here, don't even try to get by in Boston without a map, because only a few attempts at logic have been made in laying out Boston streets. Otherwise, the street patterns appear to have been decided by cows coming in to be milked. But appearances deceive. Downtown Boston's street patterns have more to do with old shorelines and early Boston's central locations for people than with cows. The northern curve of Atlantic Avenue where it becomes Commercial Street roughly traces the eighteenth-century shoreline. The present Charles Street was underwater in Colonial times and now somewhat imperfectly traces the banks of the river, which was filled in at this location beginning in 1799.

Streets radiating from a hub form another major street pattern. Washington, Beacon, Tremont, and Cambridge streets all converge in a broad belt that includes Park Street Station, an important nineteenth-century center. If you look closely at a map, you'll notice another hub, the Old State House and the intersection of today's Congress and State streets, collecting the smaller and older streets. This location obviously was vital to commerce and government in eighteenth-century Boston. Harvard Square, another colonial center, is another tangled area with radiating streets.

The grid that shapes most North American cities in Boston lies on filled land and only where early city planners or real-estate developers had a say. Back Bay, the South End, and South Boston have now been a part of Boston long enough for us to claim their more ordinary street patterns as our own, too.

Marathons. The Monday closest to April 18 is reserved for the Boston Marathon, the oldest footrace in the country. Other races take place throughout the spring and fall, usually on Sunday. The better known are the Charles River Run, the Milk Run, and the Peace Marathon, which backtracks roughly along Paul Revere's route between Boston and Concord. Racing is great for the runners, but the roads that close for the events make driving even worse than usual. Downtown churches issue race alerts to make sure parishioners who come by car can make alternative arrangements to get to Sunday services.

Running, however, is not just for racers. Olmsted's continuous park system, added to by the Brookline and Chestnut Hill Reservoirs, Cutter Pond in Newton, Fresh Pond in Cambridge, the beaches, and the meandering banks of the Charles, give Boston runners and walkers miles of greenery to tackle. One urban run that appeals to commuters is from Haymarket to Kenmore over the Green Line. Some people will do anything to avoid public transportation.

If you run, you won't be alone. At 6:30 on a cool evening you may have trouble picking your way through the puffing crowd in some places. At 6:30 in the morning, the Esplanade is almost like a small city. The runners are the citizens. The mayor is an elderly Asian man who greets the sun from the boat dock. The city council are all the dogs running with their owners. The Esplanade even has its own police protection in the coed ROTC groups who sing vigorously as they clomp along in heavy combat boots. The Coast Guard is represented by the flotilla of racing shells from nearby colleges and universities.

At one time not long ago, the Boston parks, like those in other United States cities, were considered fit places only for crime. Legitimate users stayed away. They do so no longer, for the runners have crowded out the lowlifes. What drug-dazed criminal would try to tackle hundreds of half-clad runners in good physical condition? Go enjoy the Common at any reasonable time of day. It's 1.52 miles around.

Massachusetts. Captain John Smith, explorer and a leader of the Jamestown, Virginia, settlement, named Massachusetts and New England. In 1614, Smith explored the northern coastline, which was then called simply Northern Virginia. But our coast with its granite outcroppings and crisp rivers was more like the Devonshire coastline than the muddy Virginia outlets, and so he called the region New England. Smith took the name Massachusetts, meaning big-hill-people, from an Indian village he encountered.

Captain Smith sent his maps to the young Charles Stuart, who was to become Charles I, and asked him to name particular land formations. The prince thereupon named the Charles River after himself and Cape Ann after his mother. If Charles hadn't done the deed, it is unlikely that any Stuart names would have made it to New England. John Winthrop and his band of colonists were not known for their love of the kings of England.

The Puritans were inclined to name Massachusetts towns after the English towns they had left behind. They let land formations carry their original Indian names. But these rigid religionists drew the line at some nostalgic efforts. Towns honoring a saint—such as Bury St. Edmunds—would be denied a namesake in the New World if the Puritans had anything to say about it. Ironically, their capital city broke this rule, although inadvertently. Boston is named after a Lincolnshire town whose seventeenth-century name was a corruption of its original, St. Botolph's Town, honoring the saint who devoted his life to prayer for sailors and fishermen.

When Bostonians were finished naming their own land, they gave their names to others. The Columbia River was named by Captain Robert Gray after his Boston ship, *Columbia,* which explored the river as Boston was establishing a fur trade with the Orient. Lexington, Kentucky, took its name from Lexington, Massachusetts, in honor of the doings there on April 19, 1775. Canton, Ohio, was named by settlers from Canton, Massachusetts, which had come by its name in the mistaken belief that on the globe it was exactly opposite to Canton, China, the trade with which brought wealth to New England. Beverly Hills, California, was named after Beverly, Massachusetts, just north of Boston. Lawrence, Kansas, and Appleton, Wisconsin, were named after prominent Boston families.

One notable name that didn't make out well in New England was that of King James I. His son Charles had tried to attach James to the name of a prominent cape. But James was beaten out by a fish. James's cape became Cape Cod.

Milk Street. Some street names indicate old uses—Milk Street, Water Street, Church Street, Spring Lane, Beacon Street, School Street, Old Post Road, or Batterymarch Street. Some celebrate the new republic or the new state—Congress, Federal, Commonwealth, or Massachusetts Avenue, here called Mass. Ave. Some recall the founding fathers or early colonists—Franklin, Otis, Revere, Washington streets, and Winthrop Lane. In Cambridge, watch for presidents of Harvard—Eliot, Kirkland, Quincy. Some street names commemorate lesser folk who lived nearby—Joy Street. Lots of New England cities and towns tell you where you are: High Street, Common Street, Pleasant Street, or where the road will take you: Cambridge Street, Brookline Avenue, Concord Avenue, or Harvard Street. Back Bay's streets are arranged alphabetically past the Fenway, Arlington through Kilmarnock, beginning at the Public Garden.

One founding father's name is conspicuously missing from Boston place names. The inimitable Thomas Jefferson, whose trade policies galled the seagoing Bostonians, has only a few small streets to his credit.

Molasses. This is one of the dangers in the New Englander's love of drink that even Cotton Mather, one of Boston's most rigid Puritans, couldn't have predicted. On January 15, 1919, the Puritan Distilling Company was hard at work turning molasses into rum—a traditional Boston activity and a lucrative one at that. A vat cracked. Two million gallons of hot molasses flowed out like a tidal wave through the North End, knocking down buildings and killing twenty-one people. Those who weren't killed felt as if they'd been tarred and feathered, a favorite Revolutionary War torture for Tories. The clean-up took weeks and the mess was naturally dumped into nearby Boston Harbor.

N **eighborhoods.** On the one hand, they're
a quaint throwback to Old-World cultures. On
the other, they're a code word for social class
and ethnic prejudice. The South End and Jamaica Plain
are the most eclectic neighborhoods, with a rich stew
of races and ethnic groups, gays, families, stately single-
family homes, and subsidized housing. The Fenway and
Allston-Brighton are moving toward diversity. Asians
predominate in Chinatown. Italians live in East Boston,
Roslindale, and the North End. Hispanics and Blacks
live in Roxbury, Mattapan, and parts of Dorchester. The
Irish live everywhere, but especially in South Boston,
Charlestown, and the "streetcar suburbs," West Roxbury, Roslindale, and Hyde Park. People of any color or
sexual persuasion are welcome in the Back Bay, Bay
Village, the Waterfront, and Beacon Hill—as long as
they can afford it. Artists live in the Fort Point Channel
area. Students live in Kenmore Square. No one knows
who lives in the high-rise towers in the new West End,
where the signs proclaim, "If you lived here, you'd be
home now."

Each neighborhood claims parts of the city that belong to everyone. Someone from another neighborhood
can be made unwelcome by law or tradition. South
Boston has captured the beaches around Dorchester
Bay. Beacon Hill considers the Common its private back
yard. If the identification with our neighborhoods were
less potent, would we live in more harmony? Or would
we give up close-knit communities for nothing in
return?

N **eutral Ground.** The universities and the financial district can be too intimidating. Some neighborhoods welcome only their own kind. Even social organizations, designed to help the needy or the not so needy, have alliances that exclude some people. But different races, ages, and cultures mix happily if it's the right spot. No matter what your origins, here's where you'll feel comfortable and welcome: the Children's Museum, whose ingenious secret is that it is as interesting for adults as it is for young people; Downtown Crossing, an amalgam of teenagers, office workers, retail carts, and department stores; Central Square in Cambridge, the South End and Jamaica Plain in Boston, whose neighborhood residents range over many more income levels, ethnic backgrounds, and personal circumstances than other neighborhoods in the area; and the nonprofit Harvard Community Health Plan's Kenmore facility across from Fenway Park.

N **ew York.** New Yorkers make more money than Bostonians. We don't like money anyway. New York Harbor became the largest. Its ships never approached ours in grace and beauty. New York is stylish and up-to-date. Attention to the newest trends interferes with intellectual pursuits. Life in New York is so hard that people finally decided to laugh about it. Life in Boston is almost as difficult, but not tough enough to enjoy it yet. New York is a fine place to visit, but we'd never want to live there. Our grudge against New York goes back at least as far as Isabella Stewart Gardner, who moved here from New York when she married John Gardner, shocked Boston society, and then left to the city an idiosyncratic museum in which no exhibit could change. Mrs. Jack's heyday was in the late 1800s, but Boston grudges are good for more than a century. New Yorkers treat Boston as if it were their own private campus. New York long ago preempted Boston as the cultural and financial powerhouse of the country. We haven't gotten over it yet.

Nor'easters. How Boston can it be? Observe the city after a few full-fledged nor'easters, those counterclockwise swirls of wind and snow that back in on the city from the ocean. Our tolerance for trash takes on new meaning. Our parking imagination soars to new heights. Our standards for city services plummet. Summer is only a holding pattern. Winter boils Boston down to its juices and the true flavors are all that's left.

You can tell it's a nor'easter when the drone of school-closing announcements usurps your morning wakeup radio program. Because the city manages to plow only major thoroughfares, the snowfall muffles all sounds. The trash and the dog droppings are covered. Cars can't move. In big storms, like the 1978 blockbuster, neighbors sled and ski on the hilly streets and cook hot dogs for one another on their front steps.

Then things get serious. You shovel out your car and the piled-up snow eliminates a couple of spaces per street. Now that you've done all that work, you exercise your right to reserve your spot with a trash barrel, thus combining parking and trash, Boston's two favorite bones of contention. If your neighbor should remove your trash barrel and park there himself, citing freedom of the streets, you hasten the demise of his tires.

More nor'easters and more snow. Shoveling one's walk is boring and helps other people, and so no one does it. The sidewalks become icy. The quickly accumulating trash becomes permanently laminated in the ice. Dog messes color the terrain. The sidewalks are disgusting and hazardous. Everyone thus walks in the streets, in which the snow has at least been softened by the treads of many tires. We know spring has come when the ice finally melts and liberates the garbage. In desperation, neighborhoods sponsor clean-up days. By then even a Bostonian's tolerance for garbage has reached its limit. We pick up for once, so that we can enjoy the cycle once again.

Novels. Boston is a reading city and a writing one. For those who like to learn about Boston and its people through its novels, here is a selective list of those that take place in Boston or close by, to start you out: *The Rise of Silas Lapham,* by William Dean Howells; *Boston Adventure,* by Jean Stafford; *The Bostonians,* by Henry James; and *The Late George Apley,* by John P. Marquand. Louisa May Alcott's books you've probably heard of for the good reason that they've been worth reading for many years. When you've had enough of Yankees, take an antidote with anything by Edwin O'Connor, James Carroll, or George Higgins, who wrote *The Friends of Eddie Coyle.* Mystery writers who see Boston and Cambridge through imaginative eyes are Robert Parker, Jane Langton, and Charlotte MacLeod. Elizabeth Savage in *The Last Night at the Ritz* has a wryly nostalgic point of view. Books by John Cheever and John Updike often take place around Boston or in western Massachusetts. The setting for Robin Cook's *Coma* is a large hospital adjacent to Beacon Hill that shall go unnamed, but not unknown. *The Good Mother,* by Sue Miller, has a strong sense of place in Cambridge. Also located in Cambridge and surprisingly so is *The Handmaid's Tale,* by Canadian writer Margaret Atwood. Boston's appeal to children has inspired classics. Robert McCloskey's *Make Way for Ducklings* is hard to miss. Robie H. Harris's *Rosie* series for seven- to twelve-year-olds takes place in Boston. *Johnny Tremain,* by Esther Forbes, and *Trumpet of the Swan,* by E. B. White, are two among hundreds.

Odd Volumes. The Club of Odd Volumes is for book collectors and has its own building on Beacon Hill. Boston is a clubby city, though most other clubs are not so specialized or imaginatively named. The Somerset is the oldest and most prestigious of Boston's clubs. The heads of many Boston companies belong to it. The Union Club is an offshoot of the Somerset, formed during the Civil War by renegades who believed their colleagues, because of personal financial interests in the South, were not behind the Union 100 percent. The St. Botolph Club strives for a cultured air. The Algonquin Club is for businessmen. The Chilton Club is for the most exclusive ladies. The Women's City Club and the College Club are homes away from home for traveling women. At their best, clubs still are quintessential New England libraries serving dinners, drink, and good conversation.

The most exclusive club ever in Boston was the nineteenth-century Saturday Club. It met at the Parker House. The list of members and guests included many notables with three names and prodigious talents such as Oliver Wendell Holmes, Henry Wadsworth Longfellow, and Ralph Waldo Emerson. A three-named man in Boston today risks becoming a caricature.

Clubs also may have become caricatures. Men's clubs remained a part of the era, as *Boston Globe* reporter Renee Loth put it, when men were men and women were wives. This time lasted until 1988, when a U.S. Supreme Court decision gave the Boston Licensing

Board the clout to say that if clubs did not admit women, they might have a little problem with renewing their liquor license.

The liquor license has been the stick to get clubs moving, but it wasn't the carrot. That was membership. Judging by the shabbiness of some of their interiors— too great even by Boston standards—some clubs are having a rough time. Old-guard club membership, especially for those who grew to adulthood after the 1960s, is no longer prerequisite to success; it may even be detrimental.

The clubs that are growing are more democratic. The Harvard Club, expanding, draws from a larger and more eclectic group—if you got into Harvard, you can join the club. Women are beginning to apply for membership in some of the old-guard clubs and, once the novelty has worn off, these clubs may settle down to a relatively placid old age. As in other cities, professional women's clubs have been the success story in recent years. The Boston Club, the Women's Lunch Group, Women in Business, and New England Women in Real Estate aggressively promote women's interests in business. They haven't yet faced an application from a man.

Oldest. If you're one of the oldest cities in North America it's easy to have the oldest institutions. Here is an idiosyncratic list of the oldest things in the United States located in Boston. The oldest musical society—the Handel & Haydn Society. The oldest gerrymandered congressional district— drawn up by Elbridge Gerry in 1810. The oldest military organization—the Ancient and Honorable Artillery Company of Massachusetts. The oldest YMCA. The oldest subway system. The oldest public building, outside of churches—the Old State House. The oldest animated trade sign—the steaming teakettle next to City Hall. The oldest marathon. The oldest school of architecture—M.I.T. The oldest major public library.

The oldest private school—Roxbury Latin. The oldest historical society—the Massachusetts Historical Society. The oldest corporation in the Western Hemisphere—the President and Fellows of Harvard College. The oldest public park—the Boston Common. The oldest music conservatory—the New England Conservatory of Music. The oldest pulpit standing on its original site—at King's Chapel. The oldest bells in North America—in the belfry of Old North Church on Hanover Street. The oldest college in North America—Harvard. The oldest lighthouse—Boston Light. The oldest country club—the Country Club in Brookline. The oldest summer school—at Harvard, because a botanist pointed out that he could teach his trade better in the summer. The oldest library—at Harvard also. The oldest church building of a black congregation still standing—the African Meeting House on Smith Court on Beacon Hill. The oldest continually operating hotel—The Parker House.

Old Things. Old things are a prime topic of conversation in Boston. A Bostonian's home is a good example of the art. In some newer places in this country—Phoenix, for one—people won't live, if they can help it, in a house soiled by previous human habitation. In Boston, a house blessed with previous occupants, the longer the better, is a requirement for anyone who wants to keep a social position. The more fussing it requires, the more admiration the owner gets for his or her wisdom. The more fussing it deserves because of its age, architect, location, or former inhabitants, the more it speaks of the owner's taste and discrimination.

All homeowners, whether in a classic turn-of-the-century three-decker in Dorchester, a Victorian in Cambridge, or a Back Bay mansion, have devoted days at city hall and in libraries researching their house's history. They've spent kingly sums replacing the rotted sill or ordering custom-made matching molding. They can

97

be counted on to recite dates of construction, lineage of former inhabitants, stories of present ghosts, tales of the contractor's misdemeanors, and complaints about the money it costs to do the job right. If you have a new house, you risk having nothing to talk about on social occasions.

Old houses are only one part of the picture. Bostonians feel it's socially acceptable, perhaps even required, to wear old tweeds, drive old Volvos, and read old books, preferably from a library. It's a good antidote to the high cost of living here.

Orange Line. After Back Bay Station, the Orange Line travels through places that look as if they are recovering from a nuclear bomb. But it wasn't a bomb, only plans for the Southwest Expressway, that did the destruction. The road idea was shelved. Now the area has been turned into park land and potential sites for office and housing developments. The Orange Line goes through some of the neighborhoods that Sam Bass Warner called the "streetcar suburbs," the communities that arose when streetcar lines were extended late in the 1800s. Public transportation is being used here once again to bring about new growth.

The Orange Line is one of four rapid-transit lines managed by the Massachusetts Bay Transit Authority, known familiarly as the "T." Boston's is the oldest subway system in America. The original line between Tremont and Boylston streets was installed in the 1890s—surprise—because the Boston streets had been made impassable by traffic. All the lines of the T are identified by color, a historical phenomenon, naturally. The old streetcar running down Cambridge Street and over the Charles River was crimson, probably because it was headed directly for Harvard where the color is used officially.

Bostonians could complain about the trains that

break down, slovenly conditions in the stations, and miserable attitudes among the change-makers in the token booths. But we don't. We're too grateful. If it weren't for the T, we'd be out on the streets—in cars.

The T never gives out much information, and so we will. Some stations, like Charles outbound, are equipped with a clear light. When it goes off, you'll know a few seconds ahead of everyone else that the next train is coming. Forewarned, you may be able to jockey to the best position for boarding. Another phenomenon is that once in a while a token-booth attendant hands a patron a ten-centime piece marked with the unmistakable imprint of the République de France. Ten-centime pieces fit the token slots and, for some reason, are not necessarily removed from circulation after someone illegally uses them.

Boston's subway system became famous when in the 1960s song Charlie took his never-ending ride. He must have finally gotten off the train, for no one has reported seeing him in several years. The only thing that now "rides forever 'neath the streets of Boston," is a piece of sculpture—an aluminum pole, much like the other poles people hold on to in subway cars. But this pole has a name, "Fossil." It is bent and marked with the imprint of a hand, as if someone had bent the pole by hanging on it too hard. It rides on the Red Line in car 1506.

Oysters. Oysters have been plentiful and popular in Boston from the start because, shucked and iced with lemon, they are New England's original fast food. No cooking required or desired. As diet food, they can't be beaten—it takes about twelve medium oysters to reach 100 calories. No one knows how many oysters Bostonians consume daily. The Union Oyster House stocks up on an average Saturday with twelve to fifteen bushels—about 260 large oysters to a bushel. Raw clams served on the half shell are as popular as oysters with some Bostonians.

The most famous oysters are large and puffy and come from Cotuit and Wellfleet on the Cape. New Englanders are no more squeamish about their seafood than they are about their winters, but others are. William Makepeace Thackeray, visiting from England, ate a Wellfleet oyster at the Parker House and declared that it felt as if he were swallowing a baby.

P **arking.** Americans are in the habit of believing that, along with life, liberty, and the pursuit of happiness, the founding fathers guaranteed a parking place. Bostonians know better. That's why we turned out in force to laugh as developers blew up two major downtown parking garages to make way for new office towers. It was like enjoying one's own hanging.

We cope with parking by doing without. Massachusetts ranks forty-fifth in the number of auto registrations. What other group of Americans would hold a Fourth of July celebration for 250,000 people and barely notice when the folks who run the show announce there is not a single place to park.

The parking crisis can't improve. To discourage traffic and cut pollution, the Environmental Protection Agency limits the number of parking spaces Boston and Cambridge can provide. Parking has been sacrificed on some thoroughfares to speed traffic flow. Don't count on parking in any of the downtown neighborhoods. Only sticker-holding residents—those willing to register their cars downtown and pay the extra insurance cost— are entitled to fight for neighborhood spaces. The ratio of stickers to places is three to one, and so you get the idea.

You also can't park illegally any more. When the city's finances hit bottom several years ago, the powers that be realized they could improve conditions if they ticketed cars and then actually collected the fines. Now, ticketing is a major profit center for the city. Five unpaid tickets and your car is likely to be immobilized by a yellow steel wheel attachment, affectionately known as the "Denver boot."

Unaccountably, people still drive in to Boston Proper, demonstrating that, in anything touching cars, hope springs eternal.

People's Republic of Cambridge. Cambridge is the essence of Boston. You want bookstores? Three per block. You want democracy? Paper ballots and the only place in the country to use proportional representation weighting votes for candidates for the city council. Sam Adams would feel right at home here. Antagonism toward new real-estate developments? Just try to explain to your boss in Texas how your project has ground to a halt because of the Harvard Square Defense Fund. You want intelligence? Cambridge has more Nobel Prize winners per block than anywhere else in the world. Culture? If Harvard doesn't provide it, a street performer will. Either way it's likely to be free or cheap. High-technology? With both M.I.T. and Harvard, this is the center of the high-tech universe. Revolution? The revolution never stopped in Cambridge and a new issue comes out every year.

Cambridge is a style of life as much as a place. True Cantabrigians drive Volvos or Toyotas, live in big frame houses heated to 58 degrees, and would never dress for success under any circumstances. Whatever their profession, they also teach and write or aspire to. True Cantabrigians are likely to have been born outside Massachusetts. They have come to Cambridge to escape soul-traumatizing New York or some brain-deadening suburban town. True Cantabrigians expect the future to be bright unless they get hit by a nuclear bomb, the only event that might interfere with their chances of being tapped for a MacArthur Fellowship or a Washington position.

102

True Cantabrigians give parties for causes, picket, experiment with Eastern religions, and are willing to stand up for what they believe in. In Cambridge, one slogan may be worth a thousand words, but someone's always willing to write the thousand words.

Sometimes the true Cantabrigians' fervor drives them into inconsistency. Several years ago one could observe bumper stickers affixed to well-worn Toyotas urging fellow drivers to "Save the Whales. Boycott Japanese Products."

How can Cambridge people afford to be so revolutionary? Trust funds. It's the best way to get a start in the People's Republic.

Plurals. The Boston Common is not the Commons. The Public Garden is not a collection of gardens. Neither is the Boston Garden, which is not a garden at all. There is only one Jamaica Plain.

Pops. The Pops is the Boston Symphony with its hair down. The most proper Bostonians think the Pops is a bit déclassé. Maybe it is, but Pops recordings have been the introduction to classical music, no matter how light, for millions of people who might otherwise not have had access to Mozart, Beethoven, and Brahms. Pops is the shortened form of "popular," as in popular music. It now is also the sound of the corks when champagne is served at listeners' tables during a concert. The Pops plays every spring at Symphony Hall and in early summer at free concerts on the Esplanade. After more than a hundred years, they still live up to their name.

P **ronunciation.** New England place names differ subtly in pronunciation from the rest of the country. A few rules can help. Pronunciation partly depends on the origin of the name.

Names derived from Indian antecedents are generally spelled phonetically and are easy to pronounce if you follow the syllables. Massachusetts is a good example. One that might give you trouble is Scituate—SIT chu ut. Try Chaubunagungamaug, also known as Webster Lake, about 50 miles southwest of Boston, when you get your tongue in shape.

Places named after people are more idiosyncratic. Quincy, a suburb south of Boston, is pronounced QUIN-zee. Peabody: PEE-b'dee. Keyes Road in Concord: Kize. Agassiz Street and School in Cambridge: AG-uh-see.

For names transported here from English locales, the rule of tongue is to deemphasize endings, swallow vowels, and slide over consonants: Concord: KAHN-kud; Medford: MEH-fud to some, MED-fud to others; Needham: NEED-hmmm. Chelmsford: CHUMS-fud. Or combine beginnings: Worcester: WOO- (as in look) stuh; Gloucester: GLAW-stuh. The R has rules of its own. If you see it, leave it out. Add it when it isn't there: Norfolk: NAWH-ferk.

P **roper.** "Boston Proper" is the old "walking city" on the seventeenth century Shawmut peninsula, now enlarged by landfill. It stretches northeast from Massachusetts Avenue roughly between the Charles River and Fort Point Channel. This area is also called "downtown" Boston or the "core." Some, however, use downtown and core only for the Government, Financial, and Retail districts. But the downtown retail district has its own name, Downtown Crossing, artificially conferred by city officials. This PR invention is catching on despite resistance among the populace to anything new. The Financial District is growing out to the Waterfront. The State House is called Beacon Hill, which is also a downtown neighborhood. Almost every other government facility, including City Hall, is new—new for Boston, that is—and called Government Center, which replaced the now fondly remembered Scollay Square.

The center of Boston is not geographic, but a state of mind. The Old State House is the hub of the old city that began at the harbor and ended on the far side of the Common. The Common and the Public Garden are central if you consider them the hole in the donut of habitation surrounding them. The corner of the Common at Tremont and Park streets is the center of public transportation. A sign identifies this place as Brimstone Corner, where doomsayers used to harangue the crowds, but no one ever calls it that. The early mapmakers reputedly used the Boston Stone, an old grindstone now embedded in a wall on Marshall Street behind City Hall, as the starting point for mileage, but AAA mapmakers today start at the intersection of the Massachusetts Turnpike and Route 93. This choice shows how misplaced the auto is in Boston, because this spot is definitely nowhere near anyone's idea of center, but at the southern edge of downtown Boston.

About 14 percent of the city's population—technically the city's Proper Bostonians—live in Boston Proper neighborhoods, which include the North End, the Waterfront, Chinatown, South Cove, Bay Village, the West End, the South End, Beacon Hill, and Back Bay, including the St. Botolph area. "Proper Bostonians" conveys more than geography. It speaks of early nineteenth-century sea-captain lineage and a standard of deportment toward the rest of the world. Its influence on Boston has been so potent that Boston writer Cleveland Amory saw fit to devote an entire book by that title to the subject.

Proprietors. Proprietors own some of the best of Boston. The streets through Louisburg Square are not public thoroughfares, but belong to the Proprietors of Louisburg Square, owners of the twenty-nine surrounding buildings. At the proprietors' meeting on the third Tuesday in October, the attendees vote on their yearly assessment, which keeps the cobblestones and the iron fence in good condition. Then they read the minutes of the meeting 100 years before. You would too if your organization were 100 years old.

Proprietors also own pews in the old churches. They own shares in the Boston Athenaeum. Proprietors own private ways, where only they have the privilege of parking. Of course, on a private way the city won't fix the potholes, sweep the street, or plow the snow. But because the city doesn't bother to provide these amenities on the public streets either, proprietors of private ways don't suffer. They just go ahead and do the job themselves. If you see a smooth, clean street, freshly plowed, with parking spaces for everyone, don't even think of parking there. It's for proprietors, the most exclusive group in Boston.

Prosperity. After all those years in the economic doldrums, we knew we wouldn't like prosperity. Construction, more traffic, millionaires, newcomers beating down the doors—who needs it? But we didn't realize prosperity might mean something else. Where intersections used to be blocked by cars whose drivers were mad that the traffic hadn't moved through two green lights, traffic cops now sometimes appear, holding back the angry herds and keeping the intersections free. Where weeds used to grow along Storrow Drive, some official who hadn't heard it was traditional in Boston never to take care of a road planted flowers and sent out street sweepers. When this same official then washed, yes, *washed* the walls in the Storrow Drive tunnel, traffic backed up for miles just out of curiosity. Cleaning something in Boston? It had never been done. Uneasiness now runs high. What if prosperity continues? We might get used to clean streets, orderly traffic, good management. We might have to move and found some new bookish, brickish, irrational place on an ocean where we'd all feel at home.

Quabbin. The manmade reservoir sixty-five miles west of Boston that supplies most of the city's water. Plenty of fresh water is considered a problem peculiar to western states. But eastern cities have also had their worries. Boston was located on the Shawmut Peninsula rather than in its original Charlestown settlement because fresh water was more readily available here. The word "Shawmut" itself means "living fountains." For many years Boston residents got their water from individual wells. That changed in 1848 when water from Lake Cochituate in Wayland and Natick was successfully piped into the city. The city celebrated that achievement by shooting water through a splendid fountain in the boggy Frog Pond on the Common. The Frog Pond has now been "improved" by concrete, but its fountain still sprays water for children to enjoy. The granite foundation under the newer part of the State House once walled an in-town reservoir that helped make the Cochituate system efficient.

The Quabbin was completed in 1939, displacing 3,500 residents in the Swift and Ware river valleys. It took seven years to fill itself up. It is the largest body of water in the Commonwealth and is the most prominent feature in Western Massachusetts from an airplane. The area around the Quabbin has become a wildlife sanctuary, harboring nesting eagles and large plantings of red pines. Water from the Quabbin runs downhill and east through aqueducts carved mostly out of solid rock to Boston and the forty-five other communities that tap into the pipe. Because fears of conspiracy die hard, Boston's water was one of the last supplies in any major city to be fluoridated. From time to time algae bloom in the Quabbin, making the water taste as if it came directly from the harbor fish pier. It's safe, the Massachusetts Water Resources Authority says. It doesn't matter. When the algae bloom, Bostonians rely on bottled water from Maine.

Quahog. Pronounced "Co-hog." A tasty hard-shell clam, especially if eaten raw. Also useful as money if one is an early Algonquin. Its cousin the steamer shines in chowder. Steamers are also delicious baked in a pit on a beach with rockweed, ears of corn, chickens, sausages, and lobsters. Mussels and the blue-eyed scallop are not to be disdained, either. But shellfish homelands mix poorly with what passes for civilization around here. We provide clams and their cousins with plenty to make them sick: sewage, the red tide, Canada geese, overharvesting, chemical pollution, oil slicks, rainstorms, lawn fertilizer. These ingredients work no better with people than with clams. Because we refuse to stop eating them, the Commonwealth gives clams taken from suspicious waterways a digestive bath and ultraviolet light treatment. It might seem romantic to dig your own clams, watching for tell-tale squirts at low tide. Check with the town fathers and mothers first.

Quincy. Pronounced "QUIN-zee." The only city that has produced two presidents. Famed for its location at the southern end of the Southeast Expressway. But if John Adams and his son John Quincy Adams had had to rely on the Southeast Expressway to get to Boston, they would not have made it in time to secure their place in history. Quincy

109

sits eight miles from downtown Boston, but it might as well be eighty, considering how long it takes drivers to get there. The Southeast Expressway, heading to the South Shore out of Boston, was completed in the late 1950s. Officials rated the road right up there with other macadam miracles and tore out the Old Colony Railroad, promising we'd never need it again.

Hindsight often brings wisdom. The South Shore turned out to be one of the fastest-growing regions in Massachusetts, but it was the only area in metropolitan Boston without commuter rail service. The Southeast Expressway was packed almost from its inception and for many years has carried more than twice as many cars as it was designed for. Officials are now trying to reestablish the Old Colony Line. Quincy is saved from total separation from Boston by the Red Line and the commuter boats. The problem now is only partly that the T and the boats are at capacity. The rest of the trouble is typically Bostonian: no more room for harbor and rapid-transit commuters to park.

Quinobequin. Meaning twisting or winding, Quinobequin was the Algonquin name for the Charles River. The native American name was discarded in favor of the British prince more than fifteen years before the Puritans arrived. The river was a part of the city from the very beginning. Its name is symbolic in that Bostonians have always given short shrift to American ideas when it came to planning a city. We look to Europe, instead. Nowhere is the European urban influence more evident than on the old Quinobequin.

Early travelers to Boston complimented the city on its resemblance to prosperous European towns. Bulfinch modeled his new developments and buildings upon those in England. Victorian Bostonians copied the Europeans, too. Commonwealth Avenue's mansard roofs and boulevard design were grand interpretations, rather surprising in understated New England, of the Parisian urban style in the mid-1800s. When Olmsted's firm designed the parks along the Charles River Basin in Back Bay, he copied the Alster Basin in Hamburg, Germany. Despite Storrow Drive's implantation across much of the Charles River parkland and several redesigns, the similarities between river frontages in Hamburg and Boston are obvious even today.

Although Bostonians today admire at least parts of other American cities—San Francisco, Philadelphia, New Orleans, New York, and Chicago—we still don't look to them for lessons. In the 1980s, when the Boston Society of Architects called for new visions for Boston, it cited London, Paris, Copenhagen, Stockholm, and the Netherlands as the places worth studying for ideas to bring to Boston.

The emphasis on European ideas has not saved the old Quinobequin from the very American phenomenon, pollution. Eighteenth- and nineteenth-century factory, sewage, and tanning deposits rest at the bottom of the river next to Olmsted's design. Disturbing these potent historical vestiges would contaminate the water unacceptably, and so, for now, officials are letting sleeping deposits lie.

Red Sox. Red Sox fever is a religion in this city. We live and die with their fortunes. Their rebirth at Fenway Park every April, despite the usual snowstorm, is the only palpable evidence that the crushing New England winter will end. Their disbanding in October means the end of the sun.

Rooting for the Sox gives this anarchic, segmented city, and perhaps all New England, a sense of community that few other activities offer. We pack ourselves all together into the cozy seating in that old, intimate, eccentric, singular ballpark, a bright jewel amid dingy surroundings. We take in the pulsating Wall, the soothing colors, the real grass, the elegant harbor cloud formations. The announcer is sedate. The concessions are nearby.

The Red Sox are our hope and our sorrow because they're so consistently good and so consistently inadequate—80 percent first-division finishes over nearly a half century of play, but four World Series lost in the seventh game and three pennants lost on the last day of the season. The Sox always have great hitters, good catchers and second basemen, and two good starters. But they also have slow baserunners, first basemen who play like croquet wickets, and two starters who've perfected the throw-and-duck delivery. The Sox produce the finest and most abundant farm-system talent in the major leagues—Williams and Doerr, Yazstremski and Petrocelli, Rice and Lynn and Fisk, Boggs and Clemens. But what other ball club would trade Cecil Cooper, John Tudor, and Babe Ruth?

Our memories are indelible, images that will be with us all our lives. How about Carlton Fisk's home run in the sixth game of the '75 series, the body-English willing it fair as it crossed the fence next to the left-field foul pole for a miracle victory? But this team has disappointed us so bitterly and so often that we can never wholly place our faith in them. What about Bill Buckner's ground-ball error in the '86 Series, keeping the Mets alive and eventually giving that rival team victory?

They have invigorated and inspired us, taken us so close so often to the near bank of Jordan, that we can't help but love them. We also can rely on getting there, because some of us walk and almost a quarter of us take the T.

Regular. In Boston, regular (pronounced, as quickly as possible, "REG-uh-luh") means coffee with cream. If you want regular coffee as it is understood in the rest of the country, ask for black coffee. The people behind the counter will then regard you with pity and a touch of scorn. The inhabitants take milk in their tea, too. We load both up with lots of sugar. So much for Yankee hard living. We also take our corned beef gray, our eggs brown, our chowder without tomatoes, our curbs in granite, and our change uncounted. We never drink iced tea in winter or Coke for breakfast.

Revels. The Cambridge Revels are the original Revels performers in the country. They have been putting on their rollicking shows since 1970 at Christmastime and more recently in the spring. Most of the performers are amateurs who like to sing and dance before an audience. A place in the Revels is one of the most sought-after roles for amateur musicians in the Boston area.

If you like to sing or play an instrument, Boston can be intimidating. Hundreds of groups perform throughout the year, but many of them are professional, including the choirs in many churches. The amateur groups are daunting, too. The Tanglewood Festival Chorus, which performs with the Boston Symphony Orchestra, is made up of amateurs. The word may convey the group's financial arrangements, but hardly its talent. Auditions and practices for all groups are listed every Thursday in the *Globe*'s "Calendar" section. The problem we have, if we are determined to make music, is deciding which group we'd most like to join. Lone singers with a free weekend night head for the bar at the Lenox Hotel, where everyone is invited to perform, accompanied by a talented pianist who seems to know every show tune written. The audience is as good as the pianist, because everyone stops talking and listens. Another place to perform if you're waiting to be discovered is the Nameless Coffeehouse in Harvard Square on open-mike nights.

Revere. We have no famous quotes from Paul, as we do from the other Boston Revolutionary leaders. Longfellow had to speak for him, relating in rolling cadences his fateful ride. Paul's silence is only verbal, however, because his legacy is articulated when old bells ring (see *Bells*) or whenever a bride and groom choose a saucepan or silver. Revere Ware is made by a company descended from the one he began. His silver designs are among the most-copied American pieces.

During his long lifetime (he lived to age eighty-three), Paul influenced almost every facet of Boston that mattered. He was a silversmith, which, in the fashion of the time, meant he worked in gold, silver, engraving, and dentistry. His silver is masterful and well represented at the Museum of Fine Arts. His political engravings, printed quickly and distributed widely, were instrumental in inflaming Patriot passions before the war broke out. His dental practice enabled him to identify the body of his friend Dr. Joseph Warren, the quasi-mythological figure killed in the Battle of Bunker Hill.

Because Paul understood metals, he manufactured cannon, provided the fittings for the *Constitution,* or "Old Ironsides," fashioned more than four hundred bells, many of which still ring today, and established the first copper rolling mill in North America. This copper company was the precursor of the present firm. Paul boosted the speed of ships in the China Trade when he invented a way of cladding the ship bottoms with copper to prevent barnacles from accumulating in tropical waters.

Paul was not a rich man, like John Hancock, or an educated one, like John Adams. He was more of a local figure until Longfellow ensured his national renown. His descendants are Yankees, but not Brahmins. The story is told that in class-conscious nineteenth-century Boston, those descendants refused to publicly display Paul's portrait, painted in his thirties, because John Singleton Copley portrayed him as a working man, complete with dirty fingernails. The portrait now hangs in the Museum of Fine Arts.

His name identifies a street on Beacon Hill and many other towns, a city north of Boston and its beach, and the first Masonic Lodge in America.

R **ide in from the Airport, the.** The most frustrating stretch of pavement in the Northeast. Logan Airport is 2.5 miles from the Old State House, commonly considered a center in Boston. Sometimes it takes an hour to make the trip. When state officials were lobbying Congress to get funding for a buried Central Artery and a new harbor tunnel, local wags suggested that every U.S. Senator and Representative should be made to suffer the trip from the airport to downtown, at the end of which they would clamor for funding, believing they were benefiting the entire nation.

115

Rotaries. Negotiating a traffic rotary successfully requires breaking most of the rules of the
road and the other guy's spirit. Drive into the
spinning circle without glancing to the left because if
you see the herd coming at you you'll hesitate. Once
you hesitate, you'll be unable to nose your car into the
careening traffic. Stay on the outside, let no one cut in,
and exit from the rotary if you know where you're going. If you're not sure where you're going, take another
turn around to survey the field before making a
decision.

Rotaries are a vestige of Merrie Olde England—where
they are known as roundabouts—that the Yankees kept
to confuse the teeming masses arriving on these shores
in the middle 1800s. The masses, however, quickly
learned to negotiate them, earning a thrill from the
horse-powered centrifugal force. Rotaries became en-
trenched with the automobile. Now Bostonians, like
locals from all over the state, keep them to test tourists.
A movement has been afoot to straighten out rotaries
and make them intersections. Bostonians believe the
idea to be from California road planners, whose idea of
a colonial road is El Camino Real, a long north–south
thoroughfare with few crossroads. Most rotaries, however, in fine New England style, have five, maybe seven
roads feeding into their perimeter, and so the intersections are no more manageable than the rotaries were.
Manageable, however, is a California standard, not a
Boston one. We prefer chaos.

Route 128. The circumferential Route 128
is a phenomenon as well as a road. During
World War II, M.I.T. scientists worked at
places like the Instrumentation Laboratory and the Ra-
diation Laboratory in Cambridge. After the war, these
scientists established new companies built on their discoveries in electronics. When the area around M.I.T.
grew too crowded, they moved out to Route 128, the

116

road completed in the 1950s. Route 128 is now known for its electronics industry, the millions it has made for real-estate developers, and its wall-to-wall traffic. The employment in the cities and towns along the road almost equals that of downtown Boston. Route 128 is also home to some of Boston's most exclusive suburbs and the Massachusetts defense industry. Massachusetts is among the top three states in defense dollars earned per capita.

Route 128 has more names than King-to-be Charles Phillip Arthur George. Officially it's no longer Route 128. Its name now is Interstate 95, we're told, a status that can't last long in the carefully numbered interstate system. North–south interstates have been decreed to decline in odd numbers from east to west. Because I-93, a lower number, lies to the east of 128, once the Central Artery is buried, it's likely that those numbers will be reversed. Some folks know that 128 has another official name—the Yankee Division Highway. High-tech and real-estate types like to call it America's Technology Highway, the name affixed to signs a few years back until it was pointed out that the road's name was something else. Because most road signs in Boston are wrong anyway, you wonder why anyone noticed. Anyway, no one uses any of the official names. The innermost belt that goes almost from sea to shining sea around Boston is 128. It will take many years of officialdom to erase that name from Bostonese.

Sacred. Most people have sacred cows. Bostonians have sacred cods. Cod was more important to the early colonists than other fish of its type—haddock, pollock, and cusk—because of its abundance and proximity to shore. In colonial times, so the story goes, cod could be caught by dipping a basket into the ocean a few yards off shore. The famous fish has been immortalized in the name of the famous cape and in the painted wood carving suspended from the gallery ceiling in the House of Representatives in the Massachusetts State House. The sacred cod was presented in 1783 to the Massachusetts General Court (which is what Bostonians call their legislature) by the Rowe family, who owned an eighteenth century wharf in Boston Harbor. The Rowes wanted their legislators to consider how important the fishing industry was to the Massachusetts economy when they were assessing taxes. The Rowe family themselves are now immortalized at Rowes Wharf, a hotel, retail, office, and dock complex built in the mid-1980s on the old wharf's site.

The yellow, dried salt cod is a vestige from the years before refrigeration. Salt cod must be refreshed in water overnight and rinsed before making codfish cakes or creamed cod, a mild traditional dish served with potatoes. Salt cod continues to be sold in grocery stores, although fresh fish is now preferred by most Bostonians.

Cod, unfortunately, is becoming more sacred than ever because of its price. The catch has declined in the

1980s. Some fishermen point out that fish supplies are cyclical. Environmentalists and some government officials claim that the species has been overfished or decimated by pollutants. Government regulators have imposed an increase in the mesh size of nets to enable the smaller fish to escape to grow and breed.

Scrod. Sometimes in Boston fish markets you will see a kind of fish called *scrod* (sometimes spelled *schrod*). It's an unregulated appellation. Scrod is not a species; it's a size—small. The fish could be either cod or haddock. Scrod to a wholesaler means small haddock. Scrod cod or cod scrod to a wholesaler is small cod. The fish retailer generally won't label it as to species and the man or woman behind the counter may not know. You may not care. Haddock and cod are close relatives and have similar flavor. The word scrod comes from an old Dutch word for shredded or split. Scrod was the size too small for splitting.

Seasonal Spectacles. The color brings visitors to Boston in the fall, but for those who live in this winter-bound climate, the show at other times of year, especially spring, is just as welcome. The witch hazel, though not grand or fragrant, is the first to break the bonds of winter in early March. It blooms in the Public Garden. In mid-April, the magnolias on the sunny sides of Commonwealth Avenue and Beacon Street blossom. By May, the pear trees on the North Slope of Beacon Hill are puffing clouds of blossoms all over the sidewalks. The dogwoods are in bloom in front of the Athenaeum and in Cambridge. In mid- to late May, the lilacs come out in the Arnold Arboretum and in the Brattle Street area of Cambridge, followed by rhododendrons, the gift of New England's acidic soil. The prettiest shows of summer are the perennial garden in front of the State House, the downtown window boxes, the Fenway Victory Gardens, the rose garden on the Waterfront, and the Public Garden plantings. In winter, the best spectacles of fauna are the outlined branches of the bare trees shortly after a heavy snow. The best view is at night on the Common or in the Public Garden, where the lamps illuminate the outlines.

Smoot. The common unit of measurement since 1958 for the Harvard Bridge, which links Boston not to Harvard but to M.I.T. via Mass. Ave. At the time, M.I.T. student Oliver R. Smoot was a Lambda Chi Alpha pledge. He was required by his fraternity's upperclassmen to measure the bridge using himself as yardstick. With four fellow pledge assistants, tape and paint, and an upperclass overseer, he spent the night up and down on the sidewalk. The group painted the result—364.4 and one ear—at each end of the bridge. It was once a prank but is now tradition. Every spring and fall, the M.I.T. Lambda Chi Alpha pledge class traipses out at night and refreshes the information for posterity.

Spas. These establishments anchored the neighborhoods in early twentieth-century, low-tech Boston. They dispensed newspapers, a few groceries, and all the gossip that was to be had. The most elaborate had soda fountains serving lime rickeys, a nonalcoholic version of Colonel Rickey's favorite drink. If you come upon one of the few remaining spas, order a glass. If you can't find a spa, go to Brigham's (see *Jimmies*), where you can get a lime rickey flavored with raspberry syrup. If you can't find either, make your own: mix sparkling water, crushed ice, and the juice of one lime in a glass. Add sugar to taste and the squeezed lime itself and stir.

S **pring.** The shortest season in New England. The bulbs and bushes bloom, but the temperature can hover in the forties well into June. But at least once every April, a strong sun and an onshore breeze bring soft temperatures and a euphoria that infects the whole population. For that one day, everyone feels winter was worth it.

S **treet Musicians.** "All politics is local," said Cambridge's Tip O'Neill, former Speaker of the U.S. House. He might have added that in the Athens of America, art is, too.

Massachusetts artists have built up their power locally and are politcally savvy. They have produced the only arts lottery and the most active local arts agencies in the country. Here, as nowhere else, most communities' arts agencies don't bother to put on puppet shows or gather a string quartet. They already have plenty. Instead they are able to direct their efforts toward long-range cultural planning, like setting up a downtown cultural district or funding artists to work on a series of pieces.

Several artists have become so adept at politics that they are now elected officials. Money for the arts in most years coming from the state is second in dollars only to New York, and first when measured per capita. The cultural community's success in politics has not been the result of legislative good will alone. The Massachusetts cultural leadership has carefully pointed out the economic benefits of a strong cultural industry. In Boston, more than twice as many people go to nonprofit cultural events as attend sports activities, a startling statistic considering the city's sports-crazed atmosphere. The nonprofit cultural industry—museums, music, dance, and local theater—is the tenth largest industry in the city, measured by the number of people it employs.

121

These figures don't even take into account the commercial arts industry that puts on performances like *Les Miserables*.

Instead of erecting a Kennedy Center or a Lincoln Center, Bostonians wanted their art dispersed. Several performance halls are located around Symphony Hall. Many playhouses are downtown, but several are also spread among the neighborhoods, Cambridge, and the suburbs. Street performers are found wherever the crowds are, especially in the subways, at Quincy Market, or in Harvard Square, where on summer evenings almost all available doorways and indentations are filled with banjos, mimes, string quartets, magicians, or storytellers.

The continuing success of the arts in Boston boils down, like everything else, to real estate. Artists speak knowledgeably of movable air rights and linking up with the state industrial finance agencies, for the one problem for artists in the Boston area is finding affordable studio and performing space. The Midtown Cultural District has been created to help solve the problem with shared, nonprofit theaters and galleries provided by real-estate developers building new projects. Most artists don't reside in Boston Proper, but are concentrated in the Fort Point Channel, the South End, Somerville, Medford, Upham's Corner in Dorchester, Mission Hill, Jamaica Plain, and Roxbury.

Like the availability of bookstores, ready access to Culture with a capital C is another reason Boston inhabitants can't move.

Street Picking. A way of furnishing one's home in downtown Boston, no matter how high or low one's income. A true Bostonian is always ready: One night at about 11:00 P.M., four Beacon Hill matrons were returning from (what else?) their monthly book-club meeting. They came upon an abandoned loveseat waiting for the next morning's trash pickup. One of the matrons examined the piece and pronounced it suitable. The Book Club tossed their books onto the cushions, rolled the piece into the street, and in a spirit of thrift and cooperation, pushed it up the Hill to the front door of a house worth considerably more than $1 million and hoisted it into the living room.

The loveseat's new owner is completely satisfied. She is no stranger to street furniture. In labor with her second child, she called a halt to the dash to the old Boston Lying-in Hospital when she spied a perfectly good blue armchair. She remembers it well because that was Red Sox Opening Day, 1978. Another downtown resident gave up a parking place after a forty-five-minute midnight search to carry back to his house atop his car a legless but repairable ping-pong table fit for his summer place. Any downtown resident who doesn't admit to hanging on to a few pieces of street furniture is either lying or not a true Bostonian.

Best time for street picking? Around June 1 and September 1, when residents are on the move.

S **ymphony.** Going to Symphony (the word has no "the" before it) is a tradition extending back to 1881, when it was founded by Major Henry Lee Higginson. Bostonians are convinced that the BSO, as it is called when one is speaking of the players themselves and not the performance, is the best in the world. Going to Symphony is a lot like following the Celtics. You wait eagerly for the season to begin. There are high points and low points. You follow the players. The Celtics play winning or losing games. The BSO does, too. Just listen to the audience: they cheer wildly when they get plenty of Brahms, Mozart, and Beethoven. They consider a program like that a sure win. A program full of Sessions or some other composer of twelve-tone fame is less certain to score a victory for the orchestra. Boston audiences, it would seem, for all their musical opportunity, like the old

123

standbys as well as anyone else. But Seiji Ozawa, the BSO's musical director, presses on. To ensure a program's success when he is including contemporary music, he takes care to play an old tried-and-true at the end, so ticket holders are happy when they leave.

The BSO's influence is probably one reason the area has dozens of symphony orchestras, some sponsored by towns, others by colleges, and still others independent entities. Hundreds of concerts are also given by string quartets, chamber groups, and soloists each month. All this music has made Boston a center for instrument manufacturing. The two American flute manufacturers are in the Boston area. This is also a center for harpsichords, one of the most beautiful instruments to look at as well as listen to; several makers work here.

T **axachusetts.** We believe that, without
question, we are the most heavily taxed state in
the union. Please don't confuse us with facts.
Massachusetts is below average in the amount of
taxes, charges, and fees its citizens pay, if we go by
their personal incomes. Business taxes are slightly
lower than the average—other states pay as a percentage of the taxes collected. Our sales tax, at 5 percent, is
about the same as in other states. But we don't pay
taxes on lots of purchases like food, baby powder, the
United States flag, and most clothes.

Antitax feeling has always ridden high in Boston.
Refer to the events at Boston Harbor on December 16,
1773, if you question the lengths to which the citizens
will go to ease their burden. We also look around us at
all the hospitals, churches, historic government buildings, and universities and see that private citizens will
have to pick up the slack. Almost 52 percent of the
city's land area is tax-exempt, ranking Boston second
only to Washington, D.C., the company town, in highest concentration of untaxed properties in a major
American city.

High taxes fit our expectations. We pay more for everything else—why would we expect a break in taxes?
For a number of years we did pay more taxes than the
average state. But local and state tax limits were imposed. At the same time personal income soared. And
the state, with a special amnesty program, collected a
lot of back taxes from tax deadbeats. Taxes per dollars
earned plummeted.

We're still peeved about our taxes. The real reason is that the "Live Free or Die" state north of us, with no sales tax, no income tax, and no capital gains tax, rubs it in all the time. It doesn't matter that New Hampshire residents don't expect good schools, garbage collection, or any other governmental services. We just look across the border, sometimes buy across the border, and when we've got a lot of money and little feeling for the joys of Western civilization, even move across the border. Take that, all you tax collectors.

Taxis. In Boston, the end of civilization as we know it. It's not just that most of the drivers can't speak English. Lots of cabbies have always been immigrants and never could. We sympathize if they don't know their way around. Even native Bostonians can't find their way from here to there. The problem is more basic: taxi drivers have looked at Boston, decided it's Beirut, and loosened three fingers on our tenuous hold on rational life in this city.

They won't pick you up unless you're going someplace worth their while. In a cramped downtown like ours, that usually means Lexington. If they pause long enough for you to force open the door and throw yourself into the seat, the driver won't be able to hear your destination because you and he are separated by a bulletproof shield worthy of a place like New York, with a really respectable crime rate. By the way, be careful of your suit. The drivers don't have time to clean the cabs because they are too busy cleaning the gun that all taxi drivers will tell you every other driver carries.

The shields were installed in the 1970s when a couple of drivers were shot by bona fide criminals. Now because of the traffic, the condition of the cab, and the driver's attitude, most taxi drivers are more at risk with some angry CEO from Seattle than from terrorists or criminals. In their defense, taxi drivers have more to worry about than simple passenger retribution. They're crazed because they've paid so much—some of them almost $100,000—for their medallions, the number of which has not increased since 1934. That means the same number of cabs is on the road today as then. If the mayor decides to raise the number of cabs on the road, as hotel managers and residents are always pressing him to do, these well-mortgaged medallions would theoretically lose value.

But the medallions are only an economic issue. We also have our image to consider. All of Boston is dirty, suspicious, and rude. The taxi drivers are just trying to keep up its reputation.

T**ea.** Bostonians have a long association with tea, but we'd prefer to dump it rather than drink it. Unexpectedly, Bostonians consume less of the stuff than people in other parts of the country. It's iced tea that brings us in at the bottom. For reasons of climate and taste, we don't like it as much in the summer as other Americans and would never think of drinking it in the winter. But we do like our cuppa. In true British Isles fashion, we put on good afternoon festivities at most of the hotels. Our older institutions serve it. The best-tasting and least expensive tea party in town is available on the second floor of the Boston Athenaeum on winter Wednesdays to members and ticketholders and their guests. The Athenaeum serves smoky Hu-Kwa tea, named after the Chinese merchant Houqua, the honest and sympathetic local agent who helped captains of New England ships during the era of the China trade. The steaming tea kettle at the corner of Court Street and Tremont, by the way, has a capacity of 227 gallons, 2 quarts, 1 pint, and 3 gills. It was made for the Oriental Tea Company in 1873 and measured in a public ceremony two years later. It needs regilding about every seven or eight years and produces as much hot air as its neighbors, City Hall and the Boston School Committee.

We may not drink the most tea, but several of our institutions have the real stuff. A small vial in the possession of the Bostonian Society holds a bit of the China tea that got stuck in Colonel Melville's shoes when he assisted in dumping the cargo of the *Beaver* into Boston Harbor. The farsighted patriot saved the leaves, rightly predicting that we'd want something to help us recall when Boston was the leader of the free world.

Three-deckers. When nineteenth-century immigrant Bostonians fled urban squalor, they found sanctuary in three-story wooden apartment houses on small lots in the "streetcar suburbs," like Dorchester and Jamaica Plain. The name three-decker was well suited to a maritime city like Boston. As architectural historian Douglass Shand Tucci points out, a three-decker was a ship carrying guns on three decks and had already lent its name to such other New England favorites as pulpits, novels, and brains. Three-deckers had much to recommend them. To help defray costs an owner could live in one flat and rent out the other two. Compared to today, the interiors were often luxurious in space and detail. The exteriors were picturesque, reflecting the fashion in their decade. They were well located near public transportation and neighborhood services. They were the original affordable housing.

Three-deckers, however, had a few less attractive characteristics. The house lots are narrow and some houses are built within ten feet of each other. Why didn't those nineteenth-century homeowners build attached row houses, which offer more privacy, use the site more efficiently, and can be found as models all over downtown Boston? Did the original builders think windows on four sides, even ones in which the house next door is so close as to prevent light from entering, would give the place a country look as Tucci suggests?

The three-deckers have not been taken care of as well as downtown Boston housing, but they have been good investments and continue to provide good living quarters. In any event, the three-storied flats with the stacked front porches give the city's outlying neighborhoods and suburbs like Somerville and Chelsea a look that is unmistakably working-class Boston.

Toilets. Boston inhabitants are equipped with larger bladders than the rest of the American populace. This condition results from the practice of holding it until we get home. Some people don't bother waiting, which is why passageways may emit an unfortunate smell. Unlike parts of the United States that Bostonians consider uncivilized, we have almost no public facilities. You can't stop at a gas station because this is not a driving city with a gas station on every corner. Retail shops are not obliged by law to provide relief, and so they don't. Restaurants with fewer than twenty seats don't have to offer public facilities, and so they don't, either. You can drink a lot of coffee you'll later regret at a quaint little lunch counter. Unaccountably, the elaborate, old-fashioned, and rather fanciful Common facilities are closed. Only a couple of public toilets of the portable plastic variety are available now on the Common and in the Public Garden. Others can be had at the under-Common garage. But Bostonians themselves have a hard time locating these temporary solutions. This deprivation, like every other Boston frustration, is surmountable by education. Learn where you can turn when you're desperate. Try the hotels—the Ritz bathrooms are particularly well equipped—or the mezzanine of the Harvard Coop.

Tolls. Westerners marvel: You have to actually pay to get on a road? Easterners accept it. But the Massachusetts Turnpike has much to offer in exchange for a modest donation. The road is a pleasure to drive on, better paved and plowed than most. It leads through lovely scenery, especially in the Berkshires (small mountains, they are) in the western part of the state. The planters around the toll booths are always cheerful with watered and weeded geraniums. And, like no other group of public servants in the state, the toll collectors are unfailingly courteous and helpful. The one thing, however, that the Mass. Pike has in common with other Massachusetts roads is the disorder in its signs. The road's logo used to be a pilgrim hat shot through with an arrow. Some drivers would follow the arrow in the hat rather than the real arrow on the directional signs. The Pike therefore changed the symbol to a hat without an arrow. The Turnpike Authority claims that all the signs are now changed. From what we know about the history of road signs in the state, we'd say it's unlikely.

Tonic. In Boston, tonic isn't medicine or hair ointment. It's our name for a soft drink. We also call milkshakes frappes (see *Jimmies*). People in the rest of the country might say stream or run or creek, but we say brook. What southerners call a gap, we call a notch. As people from the rest of the country and the world move in here and tip our delicate linguistic balance, some words like cleansers, instead of dry cleaners, are dying out.

Trust Funds. "Put not your trust in money, but put your money in trust," recommended the Autocrat of the Breakfast Table. Bostonians were forced to take his advice. The old shipping, manufacturing, or railroad prince blessed his heirs as they went off to write books, campaign for abolition of slavery, and found new religions. But he made sure their excesses were of the mind and spirit, not of the pocketbook. New England patriarchs set up "spendthrift" trusts, in which the heir's creditors couldn't get their hands on the principal. This limitation made lenders less willing to do business with the younger beneficiaries, keeping them from imaginative financial ventures, and forcing them to live within their means. The Boston reputation for parsimony was born of this constraint as much as from Puritan inclination.

Parsimony may not have been appealing, but the stability it fostered was. The trust funds kept the wealthy families and Boston's financial institutions from the highs and also from the lows of economic adventure. Bostonians grew cautious, but they also didn't jump mindlessly into every new trend that swept the rest of the country. While other cities were gaining reputations as centers of excitement, Boston grew in dignity. Where other localities became experimenters, Bostonians relied on the tried and true. We are as proud of our old-fashioned institutions as we are of our high technology and medical innovations. It's not that progress hasn't touched the life of the city, but it wasn't and isn't our most important product.

Twilight. The best time for snooping around in Boston is dusk. Take a walk around the North End, Beacon Hill, or Bay Village. Go into Charlestown, not technically a part of Boston Proper, but near enough to walk to and charming besides. Not everyone has closed the inside shutters or draperies for the night. Peek into dining rooms, living rooms, and kitchens to see how Bostonians live.

Undergraduates. It's a wonder that students like to come here. They can't drink. (The drinking age in Massachusetts is once again twenty-one and vigorously enforced.) Nor can they drive (auto insurance adds a couple of thousand dollars to their tuition). But they can meet a lot of other students. Each fall 250,000 of the species land in the Boston metropolitan area, making up about 9 percent of the population. They go to sixty-five colleges and universities and about 20 percent of them never go home again. They stay in Boston to enjoy a society in which a professor ranks higher on the social scale than a millionaire.

Underground. Bostonians believe that underneath the city lies a vast network of abandoned subway tunnels, wooden water pipes still in use, and secret pirate caverns, perfect for hiding hard disks in the event of a national emergency. Bostonians are wrong.

Beneath this city lies a glut of utilities, pilings, and fill, not romance. The MBTA oversees—well, in actuality, pays little attention to—four abandoned tunnels, which are mostly short inclines, and three old stations, Broadway Middle, Court Street, and Scollay Under. One portion of a subway tunnel under City Hall Plaza reportedly is used for record storage. Mass. General has perhaps the most interesting underground network because it includes the original 1820s Charles River boat landing for the General's Bulfinch Building.

The only water pipes with any interest are abandoned ones of wood discovered from time to time when a street is dug up. Both M.I.T. and Harvard have tunnels connecting portions of their campuses. Harvard's tunnels have been used for whisking visiting dignitaries in and out in times of strife. But the schools don't like to publicize this information because it only spurs on more students to try to penetrate the administrations' secret defenses. The North End is said to be favored with colonial tunnels, used by merchants like John Hancock, who was rumored to have enjoyed some smuggling now and then. But the only reports that verge on credibility place a tunnel entrance in the cellar of 452 Commercial Street, an address that no longer exists.

Perhaps the most remarkable and verifiable underground location is the garage at Rowes Wharf, where the Atlantic Ocean pushes against the other side of a wall 12½ to 25 feet thick. The most predictable underground find in Boston are rat burrows, housing, by one reckoning, more than 300,000 of the scraggly little beasts. Every construction project just moves them around a little. They find Boston hospitable in terms of garbage, but don't like dodging traffic any better than the human population.

Unitarians. Philadelphia is known for its Quakers, Salt Lake City for Mormons. Boston is also known for religion. The question is always, which one?

At first, Bostonians were Puritan, or Congregationalists. They dealt harshly with other beliefs, viewing freedom of religion as important only when it came to others tolerating theirs. But in the late 1600s when the Lords of Trade imposed a royal governor who threatened to name Anglicanism the official religion, the Puritans quickly advocated religious tolerance on all sides. Anglicanism crept in, but did not become official.

The Revolutionary War caused a religious upheaval. When the British and the Tories left Boston in 1776, they took with them Anglicanism as well as the silver from their church, King's Chapel. After the war, the church's parishioners who had stayed in Boston reassembled, but they had changed. Furthermore, their religion was gone, because the Episcopal Church, the American version of Anglicanism, had not yet been established. King's Chapel thus chose a Congregationalist minister who soon declared he was Unitarian. The congregation followed him into this religion, which held that good deeds were more important than profound belief. They did not get their silver back.

For the next fifty years Unitarianism grew in influence, dominating Harvard and the Boston upper classes. It helped foster the period some call the "flowering of New England." Unitarianism was never a major influence elsewhere in the United States. The religion's limited appeal caused one observer to characterize it as "the fatherhood of God and the brotherhood of man in the neighborhood of Boston."

Fundamentalism never flourished in New England, maybe because the Millerites' prediction of the second coming in 1844 proved a dud. Baptists and Methodists accused Unitarians of atheism, but that wasn't objectionable to most other New Englanders. Some wanted a more mystical religion and, following Emerson, turned to Transcendentalism. After the Civil War, the upper classes became Episcopalian, sheltered splendidly in the new architecture of Trinity and Advent Churches. Episcopalianism had the theological equipment Unitarianism lacked. It also espoused the social activism upper-class Bostonians may have felt was needed as waves of immigration continued. Interestingly for a city where the study of medicine is itself almost a religion, Christian Science, which relies on God alone for medical care, also found a ready audience.

Religion is still important in Boston life; it supports ten seminaries. For the time being, the waves of later immigration have prevailed. Boston is now about 60 percent Roman Catholic. The city may have made little progress in religious tolerance. A newspaper recently reported that a local politician said, "We're putting together a coalition . . . with Protestants and Christians alike." Someone pointed out to the candidate that Protestants were Christians. The candidate replied. "No, they're not."

Upcountry. The rural area of the United States north of Boston, treated by city slickers with more than a usual dose of caution. Chronicled by *Yankee* magazine. Believed to be populated by the hardiest Yankee stock with proprietary knowledge of snow, wood stoves, and superinsulation. Thought to be inhabited by rustics who wouldn't ski if you paid them, but who make a fortune by waiting out a condominium developer until he meets their price. Regarded as the home of mountaineers who, despite their lack of sophistication, can easily trick a flatlander out of money or self-respect. In more cynical moments, suspected of incursions by drug kings, Vietnam-era draft dodgers, and witnesses at Mafia trials who have been given new identities by the FBI. The newer population believes itself to be disguised by bushy beards and snowmobile suits. The facts on northern New England aren't in and won't ever be. We prefer to leave Upcountry what we want it to be.

Urban Renewal. A well-known sign at the Leverett Circle traffic jam proclaims: "If you lived here, you'd be home now." A Bostonian prefers the traffic jam to the home that's there now.

"If you lived here" started growing in the early 1960s after bulldozers leveled the West End and Scollay

Square. Urban renewal was going to clean up the grime and the crime, get people out of cluttered tenements and twisted streets, and install grass and trees. "If you lived here" did what it promised. Observe the spacious and clean sidewalks, the tall, organized high-rises of repeating apartments, the grass and trees, the wide streets with no traffic. Observe also that no people are visible. No true Bostonian will ever go to "If you lived here" if given a choice.

Where is the typical Boston disorganization that keeps our attention? Where are the crowded sidewalks that make walking safe? Where are the stream of shops and services that appear to be solely for pedestrians' enjoyment? Where is the traffic that confirms we're at the center of where everyone wants to be? Where is the dense immigrant mixture that defines our downtown? Where is Boston?

"If you lived here" is now viewed by Bostonians as the most regrettable act perpetrated by public officials in recent times. If the West End had survived it would probably now be a historic district. With its proximity to downtown, it would have been a prime location for small-scale private rehabilitation and restoration. As it is, "If you lived here" still has not been entirely reclaimed. Parcels lie vacant, tied up in litigation or controversy. The rest, Bostonians hope fervently, will meet with some wild and crazy act of God.

Urban renewal gave us a book, *The Urban Villagers* by Herbert J. Gans. It made high-rise a dirty word. It blighted the name real-estate developer. It made vision forever suspect. It cured us of urban renewal.

Vault. Some people say the Vault runs the city. The Vault, which got its nickname from its original meeting location in the innards of a bank, calls itself the Coordinating Committee. It is composed of about thirty prominent downtown business people and was formed in 1959 to help revitalize the city's economy. The Vault and its cousins, the Massachusetts Business Roundtable and the Mass. High Tech Council, are respected, at least in some quarters. But if these groups really had influence, wouldn't our city run as well as businesses claim they do and wouldn't our schools be the best in the world in order to supply our companies with excellent workers?

Others say real-estate interests run Boston. But Harold Brown, New England's largest landlord, isn't listed as belonging to any of the influential groups. Real-estate interests may be powerful, but they haven't been able to stop stringent wetlands and hazardous-waste regulations, which interfere with a developer's freedom to do as he likes.

Looking at history, we may be inclined to think that, in the nineteenth century at least, the universities ran Boston. It is true that incestuous ties coupled education and government, exemplified best by Josiah Quincy, both mayor of Boston and president of Harvard. Those days are gone.

Some people think the neighborhood groups now run Boston, making it impossible to do anything anywhere without spending months in negotiation with

137

one group of citizens or another. But neighborhood groups are fragmented and sometimes don't cooperate with one another. One group alone just doesn't have the numbers to sway many votes.

State government runs Boston to some extent, appointing a fiscal oversight committee, providing the bulk of the city's operating budget, and approving legislation that the city must file before proceeding with numerous efforts. But the Commonwealth has lightened its grip on Boston since the days when the governor appointed the police chief.

Some say the Mayor runs Boston. Recent mayors have certainly tried, and in general have run clean operations compared to the good old days. But most of the citizenry remains skeptical.

The truth is that no one runs Boston. Yet the city still is going strong after 350 years. Boston's survival and success are a testimony that all the things we worry about here—disorganization, chaos, fragmentation, arguments, and tasks left unfinished—are just part of running a democracy. Is there a lesson in this for some of the organized American cities that haven't yet reached their hundredth birthday? Maybe if you stay around for 350 years, you'll be as disorganized, chaotic, and charming as Boston.

Veritas. Harvard's motto. The truth is that the symbiosis between Cambridge learning and Boston business goes back more than 350 years. Harvard started out, like the University of Texas, as a state-supported institution, albeit the 1636 version. The Puritans in the Massachusetts Bay Colony felt that their souls might be in jeopardy without a constant stream of Congregationalist ministers entering society, and so they provided a local training ground. Soon, young men who intended to go into other lines of work also began to attend Harvard. The Massachusetts legislature supported the college with public funds until 1824 and legislators served on its governing boards until the 1850s.

Every Massachusetts school child learns that Harvard got its name from a Charlestown minister who died young and bequeathed his library and half his estate to the institution. Cambridge, closer to Boston Proper in both geography and style than most of the city's neighborhoods, was, of course, named nostalgically after the university city in England that had educated many of the early colonists. John Harvard's books eventually burned, but Harvard was able to amass the largest university library in the world anyway. John Harvard's other gift established the tradition of remembering Harvard as fondly as others near and dear, so that the university's endowment—far larger than any other—is almost $4 billion. Harvard's endowment and the employment necessary to keep the institution running are enough to keep a large segment of the Boston economy going no matter what else happens.

Harvard has always been seen by Bostonians as the only outpost of western civilization in this hemisphere worth mentioning. As such, it deserved good governance and enough money to do the job right. Bostonians gave generously to the institution to preserve the world as they knew it, and when the world they knew seemed threatened by immigrants, they gave even more. Shippers, bank presidents, and textile magnates served on Harvard's governing boards. They also started other venerable Boston institutions like the Massachusetts General Hospital and the Boston Athenaeum, creating a tightly woven society.

Harvard's prestige was well established by the eighteenth century. Even then it was accused in some quarters of aristocratic leanings. Well-to-do lads from all over New England, but mostly Boston, came to study with respected professors and meet influential people. Harvard systematically excluded the lower classes and women, but it wasn't much different in that practice from other institutions. The first black man went to

Harvard in the 1870s. It took women another 100 years to become fully integrated into the college. Like all rich people, Harvard students were considered to be models of dissipation. Stories are told about students late in the nineteenth century who lived in expensive boarding houses, ate, drank, and dressed fashionably, escorted Boston Brahmin daughters to parties, and paid little attention to studies. This kind of life led to a successful career. In the 1890s, it has been reported, 47 percent of Boston's 200 leading industrialists had Harvard degrees. Knowing Harvard's connections with the Boston business community, one wonders why the percentage wasn't higher.

Harvard became a university in the late 1800s. Its reputation as well as its reach spread. A Boston boy would never go to Philadelphia or New York to school, but plenty of Philadelphians and New Yorkers came to Cambridge. Harvard wasn't hampered by the New Englander's typical understatement. President Charles Eliot, at the end of the nineteenth century, opposed founding a federal university in Washington, D.C., believing that Harvard could fill that role better. He decreed that Harvard, with the welfare of the country in mind, "draw its material . . . from the whole country and that the graduates of the college spread themselves over the whole country." That policy continues to this day, when only about 16 percent of the students are from Massachusetts.

As Harvard became the closest thing Americans have to a national university, Bostonians lost their own private grooming ground for the young. But the trade-off has been the reservoir of good will and sympathy toward Boston among the thousands of sons and daughters of Harvard throughout the land.

Vertical. Within Boston Proper, land has always been limited, first by the Shawmut Peninsula boundaries and now by the the wetlands laws, which no longer allow filling tidal waters.

140

Downtown houses therefore tend to rise, not spread. They're different inside from their suburban counterparts.

A typical townhouse goes up four or five stories and has two main rooms on each floor. The lucky ones have back gardens, usually one level below the street. The best layout for today's living puts the kitchen and the dining room on the ground or garden level. The main entry, the living room, and the library are on the first floor, with two or three floors of bedrooms above. The top floor was originally reserved for servants and may have several small bedrooms. In this arrangement, the mechanical workings of the house may be underground in a small subcellar or in a space of their own within the living space on the ground level.

The early townhouse builders cared less than we do about access to their back gardens, because only servants used them for drying the wash and other household chores. Another variation puts the dining room and kitchen on the first floor with the main entry. One must then climb a flight of stairs to get to the living room and library. This arrangement is less satisfactory for those who like outdoor space, for the back garden, if there is one, is accessible only through the cellar. On the other hand, an unoccupied cellar allows owners to install a rental apartment on the ground level to offset mortgage expenses. No matter where the living room and library are, that story is called the *piano nobile*, meaning "noble floor" in Italian. This floor sometimes can be identified by its taller windows and decorative ironwork. Many houses have had bay windows added in front. They may also have gained an "ell" in back, at least on the first couple of floors, conveniently adding another room to each floor. A few small houses have only one room per floor.

The close quarters and high prices make for arrangements that would be unheard of where property lines actually make for privacy. Some owners share roof decks or connecting gardens. At least one downtown house has its furnace and hot-water heater in the boiler room next door. Several owners share their private entrances with tenants who must go through the owner's living space to get to their own apartments. No one forces these owners to live symbiotically. They like it this way.

These houses were designed for single families and their staff. Today, most of the large houses and many of the smaller ones have been divided into condominiums, one flat per floor.

Views. Looking in at the city is far more interesting than looking out. Early one morning, take the water shuttle or a whale-watch boat. On a clear day Boston gives forth a patriotic flurry of red brick, white granite, and blue sea and sky. At sunset, plant yourself on a bench on the Cambridge side of the river along Memorial Drive in front of M.I.T. The city in front of you gleams like mellowed brass. The best view from the subway is from the Red Line trains on Longfellow Bridge. The suburban heights in Arlington or Brookline offer a few good looks.

If you insist on looking out of the city, it is best done on a crisp fall day from the top of skyscrapers. The John Hancock and Prudential Towers are the most accessible to the public.

Walking. "Shall we walk or do we have time to take a cab?" Bostonians have been forced by circumstances to hoof it. Thank goodness the distances are walkable—a measly twenty minutes from the Back Bay to the Financial District. Half the inhabitants of Boston Proper commute to work by foot.

Before you call up visions of a pleasant morning stroll through the park, please recall the Bostonian attitude toward getting there. This is a city in which nothing comes easily, including the time-honored rule that gives pedestrians the right of way. In Boston, that right requires a public taking. Boston walkers are well equipped, however, to handle the confrontation, because beneath every Boston walker lurks a Boston driver.

Some cities try to make life easier for pedestrians. Boston does too. Boston gives pedestrians buttons, placed discreetly on traffic signals throughout the city. The buttons, when pushed, make the traffic light turn red and yellow after about five minutes. Red and yellow? The combination means *walk,* but Boston drivers have ignored red and yellow for many years. Why is it that a city with more walkers per square inch than anyplace but New York didn't see fit to automatically build in WALK for its traffic signals? Even the City of the Angels and Automobiles, which has no pedestrians, has automatic walk signals. (Bostonians have been so struck with the California custom of cars stopping automatically when anyone steps off a curb, that they've been known to stand on street corners jumping from curb to street just to test the notion.) The traffic-light button isn't entirely useless. Experienced Bostonians push it to increase drivers' frustration.

The only way to stop traffic so that you can get across a street is to step in front of a moving vehicle. Thrust out the palm of your hand if you really want to make your point. Unaccountably, cars stop. The drivers may be reluctant to face a charge of manslaughter. But they're not above nipping pedestrians' legs or scaring them. As a bumper sticker on Red & White Cab 383 puts it, "So many pedestrians. So little time."

Waltz Evenings. One hundred and fifty people, fittingly attired in long dresses and black tie, gather six times a year in the Copley Plaza ballroom to dance the night away. Waltz evenings began as private parties in the 1930s in the drawing rooms of 20 Louisburg Square. They were so popular that they moved to a series of hotel ballrooms. They survived World War II, the 1960s turmoil, and the 1970s indifference. They may now be around for good.

Waltz evenings are very Boston. Dancing has been popular here since the early 1800s when Lorenzo Papanti, an Italian count, taught Mrs. Harrison Gray Otis, famous for her husband's wealth, how to do the dance. Today's Waltz evenings are formal and structured, with few surprises and no bad behavior. The dancers are mostly middle-aged. Because those moving on to old age are always being replenished with new middle-agers, the number of dancers remains high. These are not public dances. The regular dancers invite new people, who must be sponsored by two members on a very large "committee," before they are put on the permanent list of invitees. But Bostonians are realists and, besides, they like to keep costs down. Invitations will be awarded eagerly to those who show ability and enthusiasm for ballroom dancing, as well as willingness to put on the right kind of clothes.

W **hales.** Forget the Freedom Trail. Forget hiking the White Mountains. Forget Filene's Basement. If you have one day in New England, see whales. The whales may change your life. At least they'll change any preconceived notions you may have about the relative status of humans and animals on the intelligence and humanity scale.

The whales summer at Stellwagen Bank, just out from Boston Harbor. When the whale-watching boats from Boston, Cape Ann, and Cape Cod appear, the whales seem to say, "Here they come again, let's give them a little show just so they won't be disappointed." They play with the boat. They twirl on their tails. They explode out of the water twenty feet away from the boats, soaking their audience. They move in close so that people can snap pictures. They show off their babies. They almost chuckle as they watch people go crazy with excitement and awe. On some days, they act as if they don't want to be bothered. Sometimes the whales follow the Boston–Provincetown excursion boat. The captain usually cuts the motor so that travelers can enjoy the whales' visit.

Humpbacks are the most majestic and easily seen variety, but right whales and finbacks are out there too. Regular visitors can identify individual whales, many of whom have been named by scientists from the Woods Hole Oceanographic Institution at the southern tip of the Cape, by their tail markings.

The nineteenth-century whaling industry was based south of Boston in Nantucket and New Bedford, the setting for part of *Moby-Dick*. The whalers' lives were rough, dirty, and dangerous, says historian Samuel Eliot Morison, and the whales were badly mistreated. Some animal-rights activists complain that in taking the whale trips, we've found a twentieth-century way to torment

145

them. But the whales seem to decide for themselves if they want human companionship today. They have as much dignity as any old Brahmin, as much wit as an Irish politician, and can beat a Harvard degree in impressing people. They're just made for Boston.

Window Boxes. The first window boxes in Boston were an act of desperation. If we weren't going to pick up the trash in the gutter we needed something to look at that would sufficiently distract the eye. The answer in the city that virtually invented horticulture was a charming collection of herbs, geraniums, pansies, impatiens, and petunias. The only place to put them when most people had no outdoor space to call their own was an eight-by twenty-eight-inch box outside the window. The credit for this solution goes to the Beacon Hill Garden Club, which in 1958 started awarding prizes for the best window boxes in that neighborhood.

Since then, residents in other neighborhoods, with or without contests, have taken up the window-box habit and expanded into tree pits. The luckiest gardeners have gardens behind their houses, which are visible only from inside one of the surrounding buildings. The Beacon Hill Garden Club in mid-May sponsors a special tour so that visitors can get a peek at some of these hidden gems.

City gardeners with the most insatiable horticultural yearnings acquire a plot in one of the 100 or so community gardens, growing real crops and taking out lawn chairs to relax amid the lettuce. The Fenway Victory Gardens, available to any Boston resident for a small, sometimes optional fee, go back to World War II. They are the largest and the oldest community gardens in the country still in use. Most of the gardeners sign up for the same plot every year, planting roses, fruit trees, and other perennials. In the 1950s, officials naturally sought to turn the gardens into a parking lot for the Red Sox.

The gardeners beat back that assault, eventually to find themselves one of the city's well-loved traditions.

City gardeners must contend with dog damage, twice-a-day watering, little sun, city grit, and the common vandal. The only good news is that at least we don't have to mow lawns.

X **avier.** Saint Francis Xavier, who lived in the sixteenth century, was a founder of the Society of Jesus, also known as the Jesuits. The Jesuits' point of view, emphasizing a liberal-arts education and community service, fit in well with the old Yankee attitudes, which were remarkably similar. The Jesuits established Boston College High School and Boston College in 1863 in the South End. About 1,100 boys, coming from 104 communities, now attend the high school, which is on Morrissey Boulevard. For some families, a B.C. High education is important enough that boys may spend an hour and a half a day just getting to school. Boston College is now coed, as is its law school. By graduating from all three institutions young men earn the Triple Eagle, referring to the schools' mascot, a designation rivaling for respect a Harvard degree in Boston.

X **enophobia.** Boston's demonstration of this unfortunate characteristic is unmatched in some historians' eyes. They claim that, in the 1800s, longtime Boston inhabitants treated the Irish worse than immigrants were treated in any other American city. Other historians say that one should keep in mind that the Irish immigrants—Catholic and poor— were so different from the resident population as to be comparable to hundreds of thousands of poor Communist refugees landing on the Massachusetts coastline today. Boston was the chosen city for the Irish immigrants because, as the terminus on the Cunard Line's route from Cork, it was the easiest to get to. Whatever the truth may be about the welcome extended to the Irish, suspicion of immigrants lasted well into the twentieth century.

Boston is still dogged by its erstwhile reputation, which flared again during the 1970s busing crisis. Cultural isolation is still pronounced in some of the city's neighborhoods. Bostonians continue to identify intensely with their homelands, even after families have been American for four or five generations. Fear of discrimination still runs high in some quarters. Downtown law firms and businesses have claimed over the past few years that they have trouble attracting and keeping black professionals, who move away to cities that, they believe, will offer more opportunities to minorities. But, as a whole, the city's attitude toward outsiders is more welcoming than it used to be. Like most American cities, Boston's minority population is increasing, augmented in recent years by Southeast Asians.

But no longer does fear of minorities prevent whites from moving back in to the city to live. Several parts of the metropolitan area—Jamaica Plain, the South End, and large parts of Cambridge—are, in fact, popular and have good ethnic balance. The universities are especially welcoming to scholars of all nationalities. Businesses clamor for foreign trade and welcome the buyers who come across oceans to do business here.

Boston's outlying districts are ethnically diverse enough to surprise those who think of New Englanders as unchanged from colonial days. The southeastern coast has a large Portuguese population. Asians have migrated to Middlesex County. Hispanics have come to the smaller cities as well as to Boston. Consider Kai Shang, Mayor of Attleboro, or Richard Vivieros, Chairman of the Fall River Housing Authority Board of Commissioners. More recent immigrants demonstrate their arrival as fully participating American citizens in the old-fashioned Boston way—they run for office.

Yankee. When Bostonians speak of Yankees, they may be referring only to the natives in rural areas of Vermont, Maine, or New Hampshire, conservative in action, silent in expression, and suspicious of authority. By that measure Western Massachusetts, Rhode Island, and Connecticut also have Yankees, although other New Englanders fear that Connecticut's renowned Yankees all may have been displaced by New Yorkers.

Another kind of Yankee is any cultivated, educated participant in society who has been around New England long enough to take on a parsimonious, private air, balanced by an abiding belief in good government. Not all Yankees are Brahmins, who must have had at least one rich nineteenth-century ancestor, preferably a sea captain or founder of a mill. Neither are Yankees necessarily of English origin. Paul Revere's father was French, as were several old families like the Faneuils and the Bowdoins. Some were Scotsmen like the Shaws and the Cunninghams. The Crowninshields were German. The Tracys and the Magees migrated from Ireland before the 1800s. Eighteen-hundred is an important date for determining Yankee-ism. Any family living in New England before then can, without a doubt, consider itself Yankee.

In a broader sense, Yankee can be applied to all New Englanders, although New Englanders themselves rarely do so. During the Civil War, the label came to mean any northerner, probably because some New Englanders were so committed to fighting the war. The New York

Yankees are, of course, misnamed, because all real Yankees root for the Sox. The expression may be broader than we realize. At the end of World War II, the Allies came upon the concentration camps. The understandably suspicious survivors easily trusted the blacks, the only soldiers they could be sure were truly Yankees and therefore true liberators. It looks like, in one way or another, we've all become Yankees now.

Yard, the. When you feel besieged in summer or winter, Harvard Yard is a peaceful place. For other winter sanctuaries, go to the top floor of the Boston Athenaeum (if you're a proprietor, life member, or ticketholder), the Busch-Reisinger Museum at Harvard, the Isabella Stewart Gardner Museum on the Fenway, or wangle an invitation to a private club.

In summer, peaceful places can be found at the Public Garden, the old interior garden in the Boston Public Library, Mount Auburn Cemetery in Cambridge, and the Radcliffe Yard at the corner of Mason and James streets off Brattle. A sailboat on the Charles is silent and the view is splendid. Sailboats are available to members of Community Boating, a reasonably priced public sailing club on the Esplanade near the Longfellow Bridge. The commuter boats are peaceful compared to the traumas piled up on the Southeast Expressway or the Callahan Tunnel. Churches don't always qualify as peaceful in Boston, for the nicest ones are on the Freedom Trail or tour-bus routes.

Zed.   One group of Bostonians gets infected with Britishisms sooner or later. Most have a line over which they will not go. You'll hear that the weather is "bloody" hot. Travel agents here unabashedly "book," rather than reserve, rooms at hotels. If, however, you hear, someone call the hood of their car a bonnet, you'll know you're in the presence of one who considers London his second home. If someone discusses the world from A to Zed, which most Americans don't find out is the last letter of the British alphabet until they hear Rex Harrison sing it on an old *My Fair Lady* record, you've met a complete diehard.

Zero.   A good address if the number one is already taken, as it was on Marlborough and Park streets. Addresses in Boston rarely go beyond three digits because streets are generally short. Like most cities we number our buildings beginning roughly at the city center. Boston is not logical enough, though, to declare even numbers to be on the right-hand side and odd on the left as the numbers rise. We sometimes even find it handy to assign odd and even numbers to the same side of the street, as we do on Beacon Street where it borders the Common and the Public Garden. Since streets were numbered, we've added a few buildings in the middle requiring numbers like 79A or 81½. Sometimes a bigger building will sup-

152

plant a group of numbers. Who knows where 452 Commercial Street went? The loss is a shame, for reportedly this North End building held the secret tunnel that served John Hancock and other reputed pirates during the Revolution. High-rise developers have recently taken to assigning *One* to their buildings, followed by a name dreamed up by a public-relations team. Who can find One Financial Center without knowing it's really Dewey Square? The only way a Financial Center can redeem itself is to build an addition and call it Zero Financial Center. Then we'll know we're home.

Z **oning.** The tool the Boston Redevelopment Authority uses for persuasion. Because of its past real-estate torpor, Boston was far behind other cities in keeping office space available downtown. When the economy began to flourish and Boston needed more buildings, everyone agreed the zoning laws didn't work. But no one had the time or inclination to change them. Thus every real-estate project of any significance had to come before the Zoning Board of Appeals requesting a variance. The rules would change subtly from project to project. This arrangement made much work for Massachusetts lawyers, who number more per capita anyway than anywhere else but Washington, D.C., and New York. The lawyers would sort through the zoning code for clues to feasibility like ancient Roman priests examining the chickens' entrails. Would their clients be able to put up a high-rise or not? How much "linkage" money, a sum designated for "affordable" housing or job training, would be required?

A new zoning code is now in the works to reflect current city-planning theory and to standardize the procedure. Meanwhile we have IPODs—interim planning overlay districts—which provide temporary guidance. The suburbs too have discovered zoning strategy. They believe they are too crowded and their services

153

are stretched. The suburbs are "down-zoning," or lowering the intensity of permitted land use. They are requiring larger lots for homeowners, which pushes up the price per parcel. They are discouraging office parks. They refuse to build or fix roads, preferring potholes to increasing traffic. Zoning is the new Watch and Ward Society in Boston. It's building that's increasingly banned.

Zoo.   Forget the zoo in Boston. If you're into zoos, go to San Diego, Washington, D.C., or the Bronx.

Acknowledgments

Rodney Armstrong, The Boston Athenaeum; Dorothy Arvidson, Massachusetts Audobon Society; Betsy Babcock, Hygeia Sciences; David Baier, Massachusetts Municipal Association; Martin Bander, Massachusetts General Hospital; Charlotte Beattie, The Japan Society; Phil Bergen, The Bostonian Society: Jean Bertocchi, Tremont Tea Room; Paul Bilicki, gardener; Katharine Black, voracious reader and priest; Michael Born, First Church of Christ, Scientist; Carl Boutilier, Army Corps of Engineers; Michael Brian Botte, Arts Boston; James Bramante, fisherman; Bernice Broyde, Kurzweil Computer Products; Helga Burre, Massachusetts Audubon Society; Jim Burgoyne, Cablevision; Heather Pars Campion, The Kennedy School; Frederic Cassidy, Linquist; Alan Casso, The Cambridge Revels; David Chadwick, Division of Marine Fisheries; Paul Chernoff, runner; Mary Clark, Librarian; Mark Cohen, Boston Police; Martha Cohen, Massachusetts Audubon Society; Ann C. Conway, Brigham & Women's Hospital; Melissa Coronin, Museum of Fine Arts; George Cronin, Governor's Council; Elaine Dandurand, Boston Municipal Research Bureau; Carol Darr, Machiavelli scholar; Geoffrey Davies, bellringer; Sam Davol, driver; Suzanne de Monchaux, duckling lover; Tom Denehy, Coast Guard; Joseph DiCarlo, Division of Marine Fisheries; Darryln Diggins, Brighams; Terry D'Italia, Insurance Information Institute; Gail Eaton, The Children's Museum; Harvey Eisner, *Firehouse* magazine; Jill Erickson, The Boston Athenaeum; Virginia Eskin, musician; Richard Fitzgerald, Boston Society of Architects; Tom French, Massachusetts Division of Fish and Wildlife; Rick Friedman, creative thinker; Barbara Garvey, Massachusetts Arts Lottery; Vito Giacaloni, National Marine Fisheries; Kathryn L. Graf-Gosselin, Arthur D. Little; Gail Norcross Gurnon, voracious reader; Carolyn Hansen, philantropic researcher; Mags Harries, artist; Frank Hatch, long-time Bostonian; Margery Heffron, Harvard University; Robin Herman, Massachusetts Water Resources Authority; George Herrmann, long-time Bostonian; Terry Hill, fine furniture owner; Sally Hinkle, acute observer; Joseph Hinkle, Col. Charles Hoar, The Ancient and Honorable Artillery Company; acute observer; James Hoff, Office of the Subcommittee of Fisheries and Wildlife, U. S. House of Representatives; Francis Holmes,

University of Massachusetts Shade Tree Labs; Olive Holmes, Basement shopper; Margaret Jacobsen-Sive, voracious reader, Elliot Johnson, Mark T. Wendell Company, tea importers; Harry Johnson, Polaroid; Trevor Johnson, The Boston Athenaeum; Scott Keefe, Mass Taxpayers Foundation; Carol Kennedy, City of Boston Environmental Department; Kathy Kottaridis, Historic Burying Grounds Initiative; Nancy Lamb, First Church of Christ, Scientist; Donna Levy, Massachusetts Turnpike Authority; Robert Lynch, National Assembly of Local Arts Agencies and BC High graduate; Vincent S. Linguori, Olmsted - Flint, Inc.; Alice Lopes, Wampanoag Tribal Council; Richard MacMillan, Massachusetts Council for the Arts & Humanities; Jan Malcheski, The Boston Athenaeum; Ray Martin, Woods Hole, Martha's Vineyard & Nantucket Steamship Authority; Rodney Mauricio, Harvard College bell ringer; Bill Maytem, The Provident Institution for Savings; Michael McBride, Paul Revere Memorial Association; Agnetta Mead, voracious reader; Ralph Memolo, Boston Redevelopment Authority; Bernie Michaud, Charles River Watershed Association; Donald Michaux, Boston Redevelopment Authority; Mary Ann Milano, Union Oyster House; Bart Mitchell, man about town; Diane J. Modica, Mayor's Office of Consumer Affairs and Licensing; John Fradley Monroe, Charles River Watershed Association; Terry Morris, Massachusetts Film Office; Fr. John Murray, Boston College High School; Bettina Norton, long-time Bostonian; Margaret C. O'Brien, Boston Redevelopment Authority; Jim O'Malley, Boston Fisheries Association; John O'Riley, Seagram & Sons; Pearl Owens, People's Baptist Church; Robert Owens, civic leader; John F. Parker, State Senator; Barry M. Pell, P. E., karma expert; Francine Pennino, acute observer; Ed Pinkus, Proprietor; Susan Pollack, *National Fisherman*; Michael P. Quinlin, Boston Parks & Recreation; Ron Rakow, City of Boston Assessing Department; Susan Rogers, voracious reader; Malcolm P. Rogers, M. D., Brigham & Women's Hospital; Catherine Royce, City of Boston Arts & Humanities; Patrick Russell, cab owner and historian; Nancy Sevcenko, Cambridge observer; Mary Shannon, The Browne Fund; Thomas Shepherd, Massachusetts Institute of Technology; Susan Siebert, woman about town; Richard Sinnott, former city censor; Mary E. Spaloss, Omni Parker House; Ron Story, Red Sox fan; Charles Sullivan, Cambridge Historic Commission; Kathleen Sullivan, keen observer; Shari Thurer, voracious reader; Robert Thurer, M. D., inventor; Kathy Taylor, John Hancock Insurance Company; Jean Thomas, keen observer; Elizabeth Thomson, waltzer; Rita Travis, Department of Revenue; Michael Useem, Boston University; Jean Valance, woman about town; Lloyd E. Wheeler, Jr., Bank of Boston; John White, Boston Fire Department; Eleanor White, New England Dairy and Food Council; Dave Whittaker, Marine Fisheries Division, Barbara Winstanley, keen observer; Beverly Wood, acute observer; Linda Woodford, bell restorer.